SEE & EXPLORE
LIBRARY

LIFE
THROUGH THE
AGES

Writen by and illustrated by
Giovanni Caselli

DORLING KINDERSLEY, INC.
NEW YORK

CONTENTS

DK

A DORLING KINDERSLEY BOOK

Editor Michèle Byam
US editor B. Alison Weir
Art Editor Roger Priddy

Editorial director Jackie Douglas
Art director Roger Bristow

First American Edition, 1992
10 9 8 7 6 5 4 3 2 1

Published in the United States by
Dorling Kindersley Inc., 95 Madison Avenue
New York, New York 10016

ISBN 1-56458-143-8

Library of Congress Catalog Card Number 92-52838

Typeset by SX Composing Ltd, Essex
Reproduced in Singapore by Colourscan
Printed in Spain by Artes Graficas, Toledo S.A.
D.L.TO:913-1995

Homo habilis

Homo erectus

Homo sapiens

Early human beings
The people featured in *Life Through the Ages* are modern human beings, whose scientific name of *Homo sapiens* means "thinking man." *Homo sapiens* developed from an earlier group of humans known as *Homo erectus* ("upright man"), who had in turn replaced the earliest humanlike creatures, known as *Homo habilis* ("handy man").

PEOPLE BEFORE HISTORY

When we talk about history, we mean the story of people who have lived since writing was invented – about 5,000 years ago. People who lived before events were written down are called prehistoric.

People who lived by hunting and fishing

For thousands of years, prehistoric people lived entirely by hunting, fishing, and collecting wild plants. Their greatest achievement was learning how to make fire.

Hunters' tools and weapons

Tools were mainly stones with sharpened edges. Weapons, used for killing animals and for defense, included rocks, bones, and wooden spears and clubs.

Early types of clothing

Prehistoric hunters probably wore loose-fitting animal skins. Later, hunters learned how to cut and sew the skins, using animal hair and bone needles.

Prehistoric hunters

Homo sapiens or modern man (*see page 3*) first developed during a prehistoric period known as the Old Stone Age. This and later prehistoric ages are called the Stone Age because they were at a time when people used tools made mainly of stone.

During the Old Stone Age, northern parts of the world were covered in ice. Most people therefore lived in areas such as Africa and southern Europe where it was warmer and there was more food. All Old Stone Age people lived by gathering wild plants and hunting. Like the animals they hunted, they spent their lives moving from place to place searching for food.

Gathering plants

By the Middle Stone Age, people had learned how to grow seeds, nuts, vegetables, and other kinds of food plants.

Finding food in the Middle Stone Age

Hunters in the Middle Stone Age mostly hunted wild cattle, sheep, goats, and deer, and people who lived near water also fished. From bones found in some Middle Stone Age settlements, it seems that people had begun to keep dogs.

Old Stone Age tools and weapons

Early hunters made their simple tools and weapons mainly from stone, although they also made tools from bone and wood.

Middle Stone Age tools and weapons

Once early people began to farm as well as hunt, they developed new types of tools for more specialized jobs.

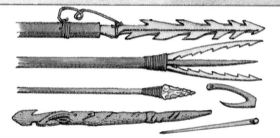

Prehistoric farmers

Between the Old Stone Age and the next major period in human development, the New Stone Age, there was a middle period when some people began to keep animals and grow their own food as well as hunt. During this period, known as the Middle Stone Age, people also developed new tools and weapons such as needles, fish hooks, and bows and arrows.

From about 8000 BC, people in many parts of the world ceased hunting and began to live entirely by farming. It was these New Stone Age people who started the first settled communities, farming villages, that would later become the world's first towns and cities.

People who lived by farming

The first farming settlements appeared in about 8000 BC in areas where there was plenty of water and good land for growing crops and feeding animals. Prehistoric farmers were the first people to build permanent homes and to live in one place for years at a time.

Longer-lasting homes

As the permanent farming settlements became villages and towns, people stopped living in tents, wooden shelters, and caves and began to build houses made of mud bricks, stone, or timber.

Learning new skills

Once people could grow enough food to live on, there was time for some people in a settlement to learn new skills such as weaving cloth for clothing or making pottery and baskets.

Domestic animals and crops

The early farmers learned how to raise goats, cattle, pigs, and sheep and how to grow crops such as wheat and barley.

New kinds of tools

Prehistoric farmers invented many new tools including stone axes, wooden spoons, sickles, and flint shovels.

New Stone Age tools and household goods

Early farmers developed or invented many new tools to help them with their work. Important inventions included the wheel and the plow.

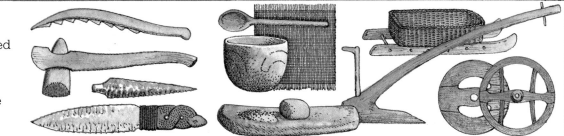

BUILDING THE PYRAMIDS

Pyramids are large stone buildings that were used by some ancient peoples as temples or tombs. In Egypt today, pyramids still stand that were built as tombs for the ancient Egyptian kings.

Hidden treasure
When King Khafu was first buried, his coffin was surrounded by gold and other riches. But long ago grave robbers broke into his pyramid and stole its treasures.

King's burial chamber

Queen's chamber

Underground chamber

Gangs of workers
Workmen pulled the heavy stone blocks from the river to the building site along a road that was specially raised above the flooded fields.

The ancient Egyptians
Egypt was one of the world's first civilizations. Many of its people were farmers who worked the land near the Nile River in North Africa. Once a year, heavy rains cause the Nile to flood the nearby countryside. When the floodwater drains away, it leaves behind green, fertile fields. It was in these fields that the Egyptian farmers grew their food.

Most of what we know about the ancient Egyptians comes from the paintings and objects that have been found in the tombs they built. Some of the pyramids had their treasures stolen from them by grave robbers hundreds of years ago. But a few of the pyramids had never been broken into until archaeologists opened them up in recent times. Deep inside these pyramids, the archaeologists found not only the coffins of Egyptian kings, but also their weapons, furniture, musical instruments, vases, and jewelry. Also found were scrolls with an early kind of writing on them in which picture symbols stood for sounds. All these objects tell us about how the Egyptians lived thousands of years ago.

Burying Egyptian kings
Because early Egyptians had no metal tools or machinery, it took hundreds of workmen many years to build a pyramid. The greatest pyramids are the three built at Giza. Although robbed of all their treasures many years ago, they are still among the most amazing structures of all time.

King

Workmen

Who built the pyramids?
The pyramids were built on the instructions of the Egyptian kings. The layout was designed by an architect and workmen were told what to do by an overseer. The work was done by peasant

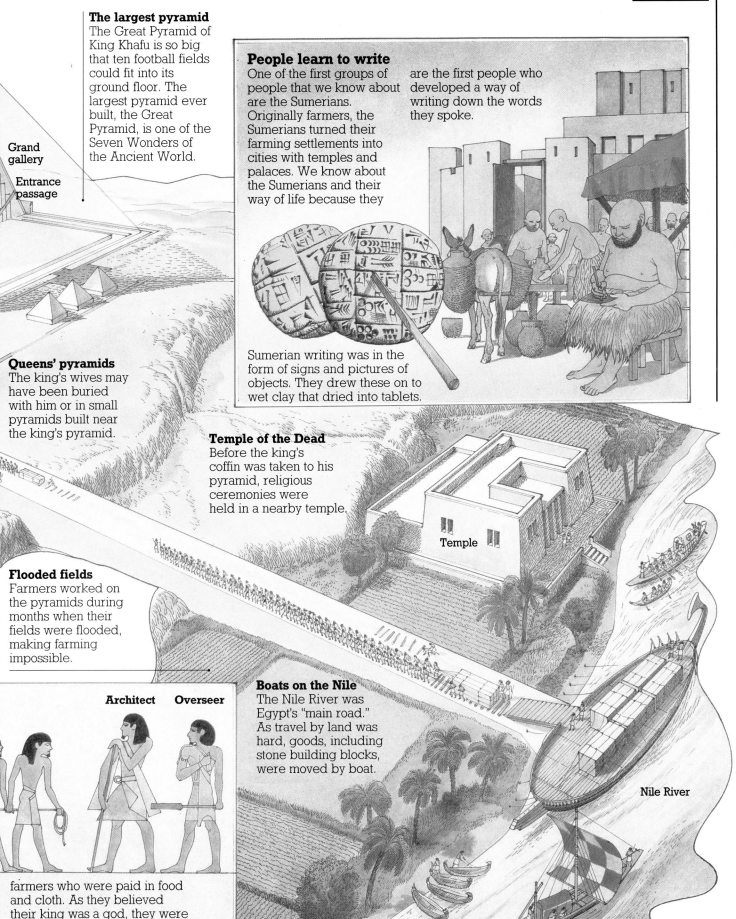

The largest pyramid
The Great Pyramid of King Khafu is so big that ten football fields could fit into its ground floor. The largest pyramid ever built, the Great Pyramid, is one of the Seven Wonders of the Ancient World.

Grand gallery

Entrance passage

People learn to write
One of the first groups of people that we know about are the Sumerians. Originally farmers, the Sumerians turned their farming settlements into cities with temples and palaces. We know about the Sumerians and their way of life because they are the first people who developed a way of writing down the words they spoke.

Sumerian writing was in the form of signs and pictures of objects. They drew these on to wet clay that dried into tablets.

Queens' pyramids
The king's wives may have been buried with him or in small pyramids built near the king's pyramid.

Temple of the Dead
Before the king's coffin was taken to his pyramid, religious ceremonies were held in a nearby temple.

Temple

Flooded fields
Farmers worked on the pyramids during months when their fields were flooded, making farming impossible.

Architect Overseer

Boats on the Nile
The Nile River was Egypt's "main road." As travel by land was hard, goods, including stone building blocks, were moved by boat.

Nile River

farmers who were paid in food and cloth. As they believed their king was a god, they were quite willing to build his tomb.

7

CONQUERING EMPIRES

Just as the Egyptians and Sumerians (*see pages 6-7*) developed such important things as writing, so they and other ancient peoples began to organize the first formal armies. The countries whose armies were well-trained and had the best weapons and protective armor were able to overcome weaker armies and conquer territory far beyond their own lands. When one country takes over other countries, the conquering country rules an empire. In ancient times there were two especially powerful empires: the Assyrian and the Persian.

The Assyrians

The Assyrians were the first people whose whole way of life was organized to make war. The fierceness and cruelty of their soldiers made them feared everywhere. The Assyrians were also masters at winning sieges; they surrounded an enemy's town so people could not get in or out. Few towns could fend off an Assyrian siege, and after a town had surrendered, its people were often sent back to Assyria as slaves. Later, Assyria became part of an even greater empire, the Persian Empire.

The Persians

Under great kings like Darius I and Xerxes, Persia became the center of a vast and all-powerful empire. Because they treated their conquered peoples more humanely, the Persians were admired and respected far more than the Assyrians.

Most of the ancient Persians lived in mud houses that vanished long ago. However, ruins still stand of great cities such as Persepolis, built by the Persians to show off the power and wealth of their empire.

Persia's greatest city
The magnificent city of Persepolis was built by King Darius I as the centerpiece of the great Persian Empire.

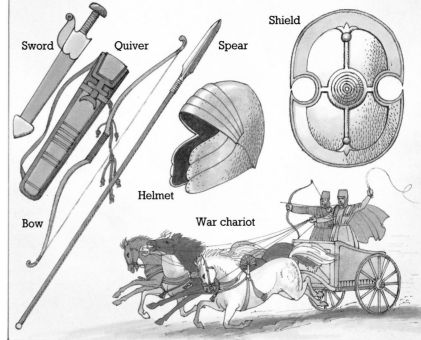

A mighty army
The Persians had one of the biggest and best-trained armies of ancient times. Although its weapons were no different from those of the Assyrians and other warrior nations, the Persian army was unbeatable for many years. Among its best troops were archers who rode not only in chariots but sometimes on war elephants and camels.

Sword   Quiver   Spear   Shield

Helmet

Bow   War chariot

Babylonians

The Babylonian Empire was at its most powerful under the great king Hammurabi.

Assyrians

The Assyrians were superb soldiers but acted with great cruelty toward the people they conquered.

Hittites

Among the peoples defeated by the Assyrians was another warlike empire ruled by the Hittites.

The audience hall at Persepolis

Although the city of Persepolis was destroyed by Alexander the Great (see pages 12-13), enough of the buildings still remain to show how magnificent Persepolis must have looked when the Persian Empire was at its strongest. The grandest buildings were the palaces of King Darius I and King Xerxes, and their audience hall. The enormous audience hall (below), could hold up to 10,000 people. Visitors from all over the empire would gather there to be presented to the king.

Massive columns

Towering over the king on his throne were 36 painted columns, each one shining with gold and jewels.

Gifts for the king

Visitors from different parts of the empire brought gifts, including weapons, ornaments, horses, and lions.

Royal guards

Visitors were introduced into the king's presence by royal guards armed with bows and arrows, spears and daggers, and protected by shields. The royal bodyguard came from a regiment of 10,000 men known as the "Immortals."

Battle of Marathon

After the Athenians had defeated the Persians at Marathon, the Athenian commander sent his fastest runner to Athens to tell the city of the victory. The word "marathon" now describes a race of 26 miles (42 kilometers), about the distance from Marathon to Athens.

GREAT RELIGIONS AND BELIEFS

Religion is what people believe about gods, how they worship those gods, and how gods affect their lives. There were religious beliefs in prehistoric times (*see pages 4-5*), but the world's most significant religions began later, in ancient times.

The main teachings of the Jewish religion (known as Judaism) were given to Jews by their great leader and teacher, Moses, and are written in the first five books of the Bible called the Torah. The most important teaching of Judaism is the belief in one God. For some years, the Jewish country of Israel remained powerful under three great kings (Saul, David, and Solomon), but later Israel was conquered by the Assyrians and the Babylonians (*see pages 8-9*).

When ancient India was conquered by people called Aryans, their beliefs and those of the local people were mixed to form the Hindu religion. About 500 years after Hinduism was founded, some Indians began to follow the teachings of Siddhartha Gautama, who became known as the Buddha. While Hinduism remained the most important religion in India, Buddhism soon spread to other countries.

Until the middle of the 20th century, the teachings of Confucius were the most important beliefs in China. Followers of Confucius do not believe in a god, but are taught the importance of good behavior in their everyday lives.

All these religions and beliefs played an important part in people's lives through the ages. But perhaps the two religions that have brought about the most changes in the world are two other great religions: Christianity (*see pages 18-21*) and Islam (*see page 20*).

The center of Jewish religious life
It was King David who captured the city of Jerusalem and made it the capital city of ancient Israel. When David's son Solomon became king, he built a great temple in Jerusalem in honor of God. This magnificent building remained the center of Jewish religious life until it was burned down by the Babylonians (see pages 8-9).

A giant basin for the temple water
As there was no running water nearby, a great basin was placed in front of the temple for priests to use in ceremonies.

The teachings of Confucius
Rulers in ancient China (*above*) were treated like gods by their people until a great thinker, Confucius, taught that a ruler should behave like a father to his people rather than a god.

The ideas and teachings of Confucius played an important part in Chinese life for more than 2,000 years, influencing Chinese behavior, education, and government.

Main parts of the temple

The temple was made up of a central building where religious ceremonies took place, and sections at the back and sides of the main building where the priests and temple officers had their rooms.

Gifts for God

Among the crowds in the temple grounds would have been men preparing sheep and oxen for sacrifice. The Jewish priests made sacrifices by burning dead animals on a special altar as they believed that sacrifices would please God.

Hinduism and Buddhism

Two of the world's greatest religions began in ancient India. Hinduism is a collection of beliefs that make up the chief religion of India. Hindus believe in many gods, the most important being Brahma, creator of the universe.

Buddhism comes from the teachings of an Indian known as the Buddha, a word meaning "Enlightened One." Buddhism later spread from India to other countries in Asia, including China, Japan, Korea, Vietnam, and Sri Lanka.

A statue of the Buddha, who was an Indian nobleman and religious teacher who began the Buddhist religion.

One of the most important Hindu gods is Shiva, who Hindus believe is the destroyer of the universe.

11

THE GREEKS

Much of Western Civilization (the way European and European-influenced peoples think about politics, science, education, and the arts) has its origins in Ancient Greece.

The Greeks also created a standardized alphabet, as well as styles in art, building, theater, and writing that are still copied today. Most important, the Greeks developed democracy (the belief that all citizens should have the chance to vote on how their city or state is run).

The greatness of Athens

The ancient Greek world was made up of hundreds of independent city-states (*see page 28*), but only a few of these states were really powerful. Of these, Athens was the most important, for not only was democracy first developed in Athens, but this city became the center of Greek civilization. Athens later lost its power when it was defeated in wars, first against its main rival Sparta, and then against the country of Macedonia led by Philip, the father of Alexander the Great. But even later when Athens became part of the Roman Empire (*see pages 14-17*), the city still remained the artistic center of the ancient world.

The Acropolis at Athens

Wherever the Greeks lived, they put up beautiful public buildings. The most famous of these are the temples built on the Acropolis, a great flat rock that towers over the city of Athens. The Acropolis was originally the defensive stronghold of Athens. But later the Athenians built temples and statues on the Acropolis in honor of their gods and heroes.

Grand entry gate

Visitors to the Acropolis went through a magnificent entry gate called the Propylaea. Nearby was a small temple, the Athena Nike (Bringer of Victory), that was decorated with a frieze or band showing how the Greeks defeated the Persians in a famous battle.

The gods on Mount Olympus

Religion played an important part in Greek life. The Greeks believed in many gods, some of whom were thought to have powers over a particular family or part of Greece. But Greeks everywhere worshipped twelve especially important gods who were supposed to live on Mount Olympus, Greece's highest mountain. These gods were controlled by Zeus, king of the gods.

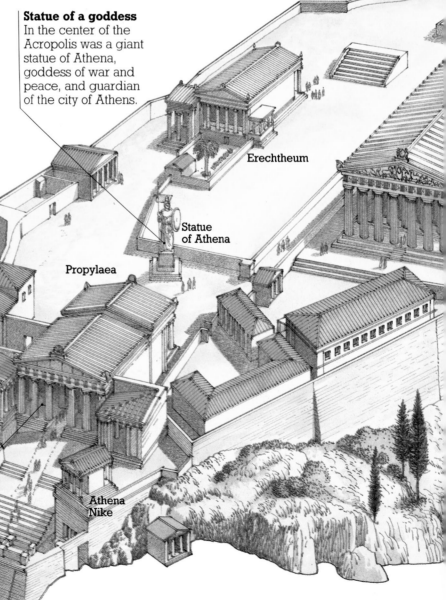

Statue of a goddess

In the center of the Acropolis was a giant statue of Athena, goddess of war and peace, and guardian of the city of Athens.

Erechtheum

Statue of Athena

Propylaea

Athena Nike

Alexander the Great

Although Alexander was king of nearby Macedonia, he was taught to admire Greece by the Greek philosopher Aristotle.

Alexander was one of the best generals the world has known. His greatest victories were against the Persian armies.

One of Alexander's most difficult battles was in India when his horses were frightened by a local king's war elephants.

When Alexander died of fever at age 33, he had not only won an empire but had taken the Greek way of life to many other countries.

A hero's temple
Near the Parthenon was the Erechtheum, a temple built to honor a legendary Greek hero called Erechtheus, whom the Athenians worshipped as a god.

Watching a play
Greek theaters were built so that people in the highest seats could hear just as well as those in the front rows. The actors performed in the orchestra area or from the steps of the building behind. In Greek theater, all the actors wore masks on their faces and all the women's parts were played by men.

Parthenon

Orchestra

Theater of Dionysus

The most famous Greek temple
The Parthenon, the greatest of Athens temples, was built in honor of the goddess Athena. In later times, the Parthenon became a Christian church and then a Muslim mosque.

The Greek theater
The first great plays were written by the Greeks to be acted in their theaters. Near the Acropolis, a theater was built to honor the god Dionysus, patron of music, dancing, and the theater. Twice a year plays were performed at the theater during special festivals held in honor of Dionysus.

The best plays
At a theater festival the audience watched one new play after another. At the end, prizes were given to the best writer, play producer, and actor.

THE ROMAN EMPIRE

The ancient Romans believed that Rome was founded by two brothers called Romulus and Remus, whose father was Mars, the god of war. We now know that Rome began as a small village on one of seven hills in the center of Italy. In time, this village joined up with villages on the other six hills to become one big city called Rome.

From a republic to an empire

Early Rome was ruled by unpopular kings. Later, it became a republic with a senate – a gathering of noblemen who were elected by the wealthiest citizens to organize the government and the army. Julius Caesar was a successful general and politician. Because some Roman senators felt that he was becoming too powerful – almost like a king – he was assassinated.

The first Roman emperor was a grand-nephew of Julius Caesar, named Octavian. He changed his name to Augustus and ruled for nearly 50 years, bringing peace and prosperity after years of war.

The Roman army

Tough, brave fighters, the Romans made very good soldiers. Having conquered the whole of Italy, the Roman army then marched into other countries and defeated their armies. At its largest, the Roman Empire included all the countries around the Mediterranean Sea and stretched as far as Britain in the north and Arabia in the southwest.

Roman soldiers not only fought battles, they were also trained to build roads, bridges, and new towns. Each soldier stayed in the army for 20 or 25 years. When he left the army, he was given land to farm in the country he had helped to conquer. In this way the Roman style of living spread throughout their huge empire.

Town and country life in Roman times

In this illustration, you can see an imaginary Roman town in southern Europe. Houses and shops are grouped around important places such as temples, government buildings, public baths, and places of entertainment. The picture is continued across the page and there Roman soldiers are guarding slaves who are building a new road. The land below the road belongs to a farming estate that is growing food for people in the town.

Flax for linen
Flax plants were grown in marshes near the town. The flax fiber was used for weaving linen into cloth.

Places of entertainment
Bear-baiting, cock-fighting, and acrobatic displays were performed in amphitheaters. These shows were more humble than the ones put on in Rome, which involved trained fighters, called gladiators, who fought each other or wild animals. At theaters, people enjoyed music, dancing, and plays.

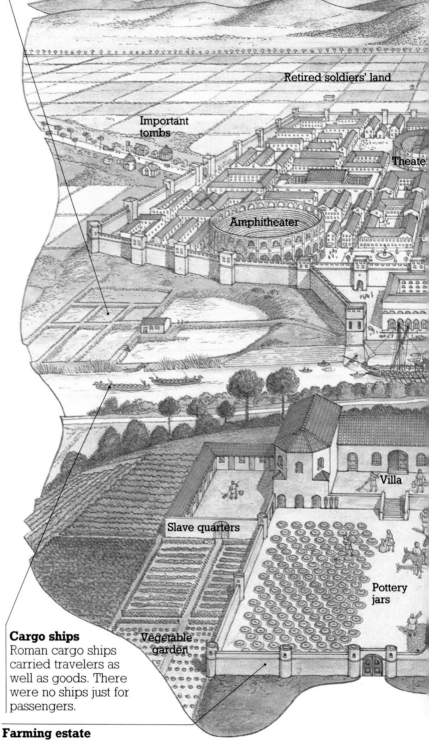

Retired soldiers' land

Important tombs

Theater

Amphitheater

Villa

Slave quarters

Pottery jars

Vegetable garden

Cargo ships
Roman cargo ships carried travelers as well as goods. There were no ships just for passengers.

Farming estate
Rich men often owned country estates that were looked after for them by farmers who paid them rent. Most of the work was done by slaves. The estate owner lived with his family in a big house called a villa. The family had their own temple to worship in. Nearby were orchards, grapevines for wine, and a vegetable garden. Pottery jars, half buried in the courtyard, kept food from going bad.

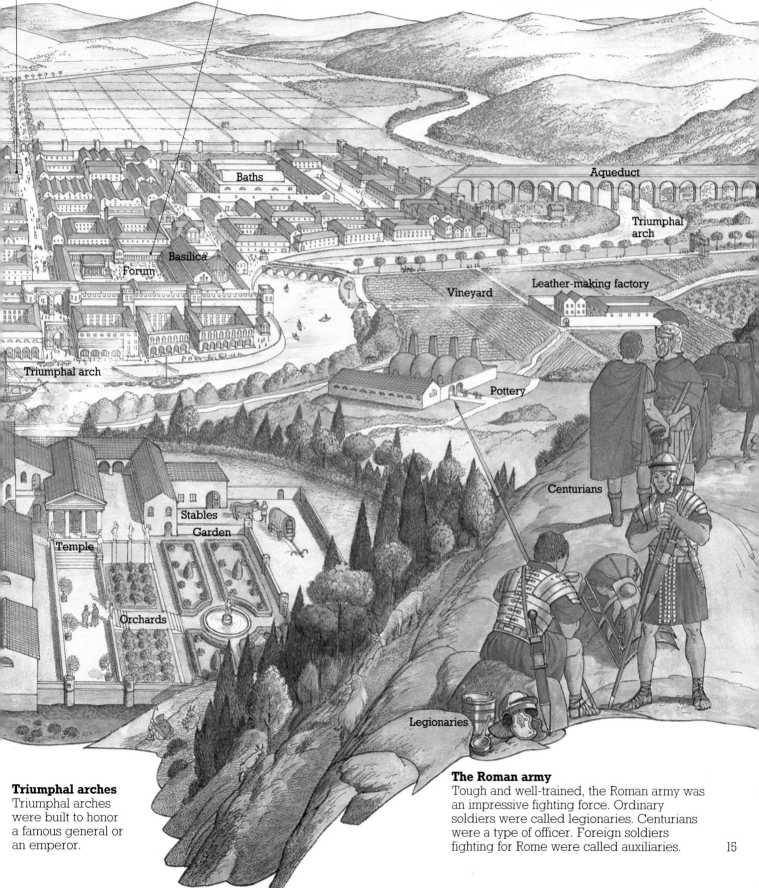

Worshipping the gods
Important gods such as Jupiter, king of the gods, had temples built in their honor in the town center. Smaller temples for less important gods were erected in other parts of the town.

Town center
The busiest part of any Roman town was the forum. This was where government buildings such as the basilica, or town hall, could be found. In the forum, there were also shops and market stalls where people could buy and sell goods.

Bathing and swimming
Every town had public baths for bathing and swimming. Some bathrooms had warm water heated by underfloor furnaces. The furnaces also sent warm air through the rooms to give an early kind of central heating.

Baths

Aqueduct

Triumphal arch

Basilica

Forum

Vineyard

Leather-making factory

Triumphal arch

Pottery

Temple

Stables

Garden

Centurians

Orchards

Legionaries

Triumphal arches
Triumphal arches were built to honor a famous general or an emperor.

The Roman army
Tough and well-trained, the Roman army was an impressive fighting force. Ordinary soldiers were called legionaries. Centurians were a type of officer. Foreign soldiers fighting for Rome were called auxiliaries.

15

Empty villages
In parts of the empire were empty villages that had once belonged to the local people. People left their old houses to work for the Romans. They often worked as laborers living in huts near the farming estates.

Stone quarries
Slaves worked in quarries digging out stone and slate. The stone was then taken in ox-drawn carts to where roads, houses, and bridges were being built by other slave workers.

Fresh water supply
In order to get fresh water into their towns, the Romans built aqueducts. These were bridges with tunnels through which the water flowed. After leaving the aqueduct, the water ran through underground lead pipes into the town.

Aqueduct and bridge

Farm laborers' huts

Auxiliaries

Slave workers

IMP. CA
DIVI AL
VIAM
ARELA
GLANV
XXII

Slaves and citizens
Slaves did most of the hardest work in the empire and had little freedom. Roman citizens, whether rich or poor, were free to live and work as they wished.

Milestones
Stone pillars were put up at the side of the road to show the distance between each town.

Building new roads
Originally the Romans built new roads for their soldiers to march on between their camps and forts. Later, the roads were used by everyone who traveled in the Roman Empire. The roads were carefully laid out in plans made by a surveyor. He used an instrument called a groma to help him keep the line of the road straight.

16

Building bridges

Strong, well-made bridges of wood or stone were often built across rivers in order to link the new Roman roads.

Wood for burning

The Romans cut down the woods and forests near towns. The wood was cut up in wood yards by slaves and then taken to the town and country estates to be used as fuel for cooking and heating.

Timber yard

Crane

Gold mine

Road-building engineer

Groma

Digging for gold

In the mines, gold and other metals were dug up by slaves working in terrible conditions.

Surveyor

Town life

Throughout their empire the Romans built towns and cities in places where there had once only been villages or empty countryside. Most of the towns were planned to look like Rome. The town center was called the forum. Here important places such as government buildings and temples were grouped together. The edges of the forum were surrounded by shops and market stalls.

Houses, places of entertainment, and smaller temples were built in other parts of the town. The streets of a Roman town were always full of people carrying goods and going to and from work and school. Among the crowd were soldiers, slaves, and visitors from other parts of the empire.

Country life

As soon as the Romans took over new lands, they built roads and bridges. When they decided to stay in a particular area, they cleared the surrounding countryside and built a town and some farms.

Farming was a very important part of Roman life, since food was always needed to feed the army and people in the towns and cities. Although some farms were quite small, others were big estates where the work was done by hundreds of slaves.

Most people who lived in the country led hard lives, working all day in the fields, clearing the forests, and digging in the mines and quarries. Only the rich Romans who lived in grand country houses called villas led pleasant lives. Although some of them supervised their big estates, they all had plenty of free time to enjoy a peaceful life away from the busy towns.

The breakup of the empire

After many years of ruling their lands successfully, the Romans began to have trouble. The army had to put down riots and rebellions within the empire. At the same time, tribes who lived outside the empire, whom the Romans called barbarians, were making attacks on Roman towns and farms.

Eventually the emperor decided it might be easier to govern the empire if it was split into two parts, an eastern empire and a western empire. The eastern empire lasted for many years, but the western empire was destroyed by the barbarian tribes.

Nearly 450 years after Augustus became the first emperor, a barbarian tribe called the Visigoths conquered Italy. The city of Rome was burned and much of the Roman Empire was destroyed.

THE BARBARIAN INVASIONS

The name "barbarian," given by the Romans to German tribesmen who invaded their empire, meant a person whose speech the Romans could not understand. Many people think of the barbarians only as destroyers of the Greek and Roman way of life. Although they were certainly tough warriors, they were also successful farmers and traders and magnificent craftsmen. The barbarians also adopted many Roman ideas that they admired, including the Christian religion.

Christians are people who believe that Jesus Christ was the Son of God. Most of what we know about Jesus' life comes from the part of the Bible known as the New Testament. Within a few years of Jesus' death, small groups of Christians were spreading Jesus' ideas and within 300 years, Christianity had not only become the main religion of the Roman Empire but the Christian Church had become rich and powerful.

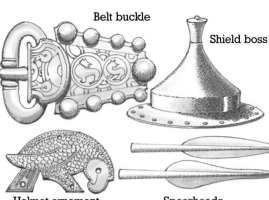

Belt buckle

Shield boss

Helmet ornament

Spearheads

Ornaments and weapons

The German tribesmen were skillful craftsmen, as can be seen from the brass ornaments on their helmets and belts, and the careful workmanship in their spears and shield bosses (the knobs on the front of shields).

A great war leader

The Huns destroyed many Roman towns and forts, led by their great leader Attila, who was known as the "Scourge of God."

Warriors in the barbarian armies

Warriors in the German tribes were neither as well-trained nor equipped as the Roman soldiers they fought against. But many leaders of the tribes knew how to defeat the Romans because they had served as auxiliary soldiers in the Roman army. The most destructive of the barbarian tribes were not the Germans from the north of Europe, but the Huns, warriors who rode into Europe from Asia, spreading terror wherever they went.

Invaders of the Roman Empire

German tribesmen called Goths had been causing trouble along the borders of the Roman Empire for many years. The Goths eventually split into two main groups, the Visigoths (West Goths) and the Ostrogoths (East Goths). The Visigoths did most to bring about the collapse of the Roman Empire by invading Italy and other important parts of the empire.

Fierce nomads

The Huns were nomads, tribesmen who moved from place to place to find food. Brilliant warriors on horseback, the Huns swept into parts of the Roman Empire from Asia, terrorizing the people in their path.

Sword hilts

Ax heads

German swords and axes

Swords were usually only carried by kings and important warriors. Vicious-looking axes that were thrown at an enemy from close range were popular weapons with the Franks. In later times they used heavier battle-axes.

Invaders from across the sea

German tribes not only moved into other countries in mainland Europe, but also across the sea to Britain. About 1500 years ago, three German tribes, the Saxons, Angles and Jutes, invaded and settled in southern Britain. The German tribes divided the lands they conquered into seven kingdoms that lasted until the Norman Conquest (*see pages 22-23*). The name "England" comes from the area belonging to the Angles, known as Angle land or Engla land.

Friends and enemies

Franks were German tribesmen who had been allies of the Romans until they began invading the Roman Empire.

Barbarians who became Christians

The first barbarian leader to become a Christian was Clovis, King of the Franks, who conquered a part of the Roman Empire called Gaul. By the time Clovis died, the Franks had such a strong hold on Gaul that the country was renamed "France" after them.

The early Christians

At first the Romans disliked Christians, whom they thought were troublemakers. Some Christians were even thrown to lions in the Roman circus.

Constantine was the first Roman emperor to become a Christian. He made Christianity the official religion of the Roman Empire.

One leader of the early Church was St. Augustine. He became bishop of Hippo in North Africa and his ideas inspired many other saints and scholars.

Charlemagne, King of the Franks, was crowned Roman emperor after he had united much of Europe and made it a great Christian empire.

THE SPREAD OF CHRISTIANITY

From the beginnings of the Christian religion (*see pages 18-19*), some people believed they would be better Christians if they went away on their own into wild country and lived a simple life, praying to and thinking about God. These men became known as monks (from the Greek word for "alone"). During the AD 300s, while some monks still preferred to live alone, others began to live together in communities called monasteries. Women also began to live together in religious communities called convents and were known as nuns.

By the AD 500s monasteries had been built all over Europe. Many of the communities living in them (called religious orders) followed the guidelines for monastery life suggested by St. Benedict, an Italian monk. St. Benedict said that monks should think of the other monks as their second family with the head monk or abbot as their second father. St. Benedict's Rule also set down how a monk should organize his day between work and prayer.

The great age of the monasteries

The barbarian tribes who took over parts of the Roman Empire (*see pages 18-19*) had their own gods and at first they did not want to know about Christianity, the religion of Rome. Many brave monks worked among them as missionaries, including St. Columbanus, from Ireland, who founded monasteries at Luxeuil in France and Bobbio in Italy.

Monasteries became places that looked after the poor and sick, and important centers of learning, where books were written. For many years, monks were the only people who could read and write. Since they were the teachers and the historians, much of what we know about the past is due to their scholarly work.

Although many monasteries and convents were ruined by events such as the Viking raids (*see pages 22-23*) and the Black Death (*see pages 26-27*), monks and nuns continued to play an important part in European life for hundreds of years.

Although some orders of monks lived in quite simple abbeys or monasteries, other monks lived in large communities that owned a lot of land. Fountains Abbey in the north of England (right) was built by Cistercian monks. Cistercians always built their abbeys in the countryside where they could work the land.

Muslims and Islam

Muslims are people who believe in Islam, a religion begun by the great teacher Muhammad in the AD 600s. Like Christians and Jews, Muslims believe in only one God, whom they call Allah. The first followers of Islam, the Arabs, soon spread their religion by conquering countries in Asia, North Africa, and Europe. Every country that became part of the Muslim Empire benefited from the Arabs' advanced knowledge of medicine, science, and the arts.

Arab warriors

Monk

Friar

Abbot

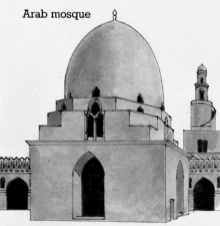

Arab mosque

Mosques, the places where Muslims worship, are among the most beautifully designed Arab buildings.

After Muhammad's death, the Arabs began to fight "holy" wars that would take Islam into non-Islamic countries.

Living religious lives

Monks promised to give up their possessions, never to marry, and to obey their superiors, who included the abbot, or chief monk, in the monastery. Friars had no fixed homes and moved around the country preaching and helping those in need.

Eating and sleeping quarters
The monks ate in the refectory and slept in the dormitory. The lay brothers, religious men who were not true monks but who lived in the monastery and helped with the work, had their own separate rooms.

Center of monastic life
The most important of all the monastery buildings was the church where the monks prayed and sang in the choir.

A peaceful walkway
Vegetables were often grown in the center square of the covered walkway or cloisters.

Church

Lay brothers' dormitory

Cloisters

Lay brothers' refectory

Infirmary

Monks' refectory

Abbot's house

Monks' dormitory

Growing food
Monasteries grew nearly all their own food. Some orders of monks, such as the Cistercians, became experts in farming and forestry.

Daily work
Besides working the fields and kitchen gardens, monks also worked in the kitchens, bakehouse, stables, and workshops. Some monks worked in the library, binding, copying, and illustrating books.

Caring for the sick
Most of the earliest hospitals were started by monks or nuns. Caring for the old and sick was an important part of religious peoples' work, so a monastery always had a large hospital or infirmary.

21

THE VIKINGS

About 400 years after German tribesmen invaded the Roman Empire (*see pages 18-19*), new bands of fierce warriors began to appear in parts of Europe. These raiders, who came from northern countries now called Denmark, Norway and Sweden, were known as Norsemen or, in later times, Vikings, a name meaning "sea pirates."

Although most Vikings made their living from farming, they were also people of the sea, traveling long distances to trade and explore new lands.

At first the Vikings raided other countries in order to steal sheep, cattle, and other kinds of food, and to plunder such places as monasteries of their riches. The Vikings were greatly feared because they would suddenly appear from the sea without warning. Churches were looted, villages were robbed of their animals and stores, and people were carried off by the Vikings to be sold as slaves.

After many years as raiders, the Vikings began to look for new farmland and places to settle outside their own countries. Waves of Viking invaders landed in parts of England, Scotland, Ireland, Holland, Germany, and France. It was the Vikings or Norsemen who settled on the coast of northern France and became known as the Normans, who were the next, and final, conquerors of England.

Ships for warriors
Known as longships, Viking warships were built for speed. The front end often had a carved dragon's head.

Trading ships
The Vikings were expert shipbuilders. Most of the ships they built were merchant ships, used for carrying goods across the seas when they went on raids or on trading expeditions.

Anglo-Saxon village

Anglo-Saxons were German tribespeople who settled in Britain (*see pages 18-19*). Most Anglo-Saxons lived in small farming settlements protected by a stockade that kept out enemies and wild animals. The peasants lived in huts grouped around larger buildings belonging to nobles.

Viking raiders
There were two kinds of Viking raids. Sometimes the warbands returned quickly to their boats, taking as many valuables and cattle as they could manage back to their homelands. But other raiding parties came not only to steal from the local people but also to look for new farmland where they and their families could settle.

Easy ships to land
The ships were so light and shallow, they could sail up rivers or be easily dragged ashore.

Surprise attacks
The Vikings usually landed in small bands on unprotected beaches or riverbanks. The warbands then moved inland, robbing and burning any local settlements or monasteries.

Weapons and armor
Viking warriors' chief weapons were spears, swords, and broad-axes. They protected themselves with shields and by wearing metal or leather helmets.

"Fury of the Norsemen"
A Viking raid was such a terrifying experience for townspeople, farmers, and monks that a special prayer was said in Christian churches in parts of Europe that began "God deliver us from the fury of the Norsemen."

The Norman Conquest

When Harold, Earl of Wessex, visited William of Normandy in France, he promised to help William become king of England.

But when the English king, Edward, died, Harold was chosen king. William then led an army of 5,000 men across the sea to England.

At the Battle of Hastings King Harold was defeated and killed by the Normans. William and his army then conquered Saxon England.

William became king of England and built castles to defend his new country. One famous Norman castle is the White Tower in London.

23

KNIGHTS AND CRUSADERS

Although there had been soldiers called knights in ancient times, knights became more important in the years following the Norman Conquest (*see pages 22-23*). Some knights were rich landowners or the sons of lords. Others were made knights as a reward for fighting well in battle. It became the knight's job to find men to fight for the king in wartime. Knights were also meant to be good Christians and to defend the Christian Church against its enemies.

The wars of the Crusades

Christian pilgrims had always visited places in the Holy Land that were told of in the Bible. During the AD 600s, the Holy Land had been conquered by Muslims (*see pages 20-21*). When the Christian pilgrims came into conflict with the Muslims who lived there, armies were sent from Europe to recapture the Holy Land from the Muslims. The wars that took place between the Christian armies and the Muslim armies were called the Crusades, and the knights and ordinary soldiers who fought in the Christian armies were called Crusaders.

Although the Crusaders won some important victories in the Holy Land, their leaders often quarreled and they never had enough troops to hold on to the land they captured. After a number of Crusades, the Christians stopped trying to recapture the Holy Land and their armies returned to Europe, leaving the area to the people who lived there.

Attack and defense during the Crusades

The battles fought between the Crusaders and their Muslim enemies were both bigger and better planned than battles in earlier wars. These pictures show how castles were built, and how weapons and armor were specially made, so that the soldiers of both sides could either attack or defend important places in the Holy Land.

Body defense
Crusader knights were often protected from head to toe in armor called chain mail. Made of linked steel rings, chain mail must have been hot and uncomfortable.

Fierce warriors
The Muslims fought the heavily armed Crusaders with daggers, light swords, and short bows. Brilliant horsemen, the Muslims could carry out lightning attacks riding their fast ponies.

A mighty fortress
Krak des Chevaliers was the strongest and most important castle that the Crusaders built in the Holy Land. Once they commanded strongholds like this, small numbers of Crusaders could keep control of the country nearby and survive sieges from large Muslim armies. Krak des Chevaliers was besieged for a year before it surrendered.

Siege weapons
The Crusaders learned a great deal about siege weapons from the Muslims. A giant rock-throwing catapult called "Bad Neighbor" helped the Crusaders capture the Muslim town of Acre.

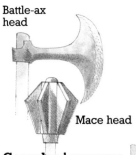

Battle-ax head

Mace head

Crusaders' weapons
The most important weapon was a sword, but knights also used axes, lances, and maces (a type of club).

Dangerous games
During peacetime, some knights took part in mock battles called tournaments. These battles were fought on horseback with a blunt spear and sword. Each individual fight during the tournament was called a joust. Tournaments could be extremely dangerous and knights were often injured or killed. But they were very popular with the crowds who came to watch, including ladies and other knights.

Riding into battle
Powerful war-horses carried knights into battle. Many knights were soldier-monks, fighting only for the Christian Church. This group of Crusaders had crosses sewn on to their tunics to identify them.

Knight's sword   Crusader's shield

25

WAR AND PLAGUE

England and France had been at war many times since William the Conqueror had invaded England (*see pages 22-23*). The longest series of wars between them took place in France and became known as the Hundred Years War.

The war started when the English king, Edward III, whose mother was French, claimed the right to be King of France. English kings had once controlled large areas of France, which had been given to them in the 1100s when Henry II of England married a French queen. But by the start of the Hundred Years War, England had lost control of all its French territory except an area called Gascony.

The English armies had two successful periods during the Hundred Years War, once when they were led by Edward III, and later by another warrior king, Henry V. Although both kings had far fewer troops than the French, they were both excellent generals and made clever use of the skills of the English longbowmen. In two important English victories, at the battles of Crécy and Agincourt, the English archers defeated far larger French armies mostly made up of armored knights on horseback.

But the English never had enough soldiers or supplies to keep on winning, and in between the English victories, the French won back control of their country. By the end of the war, England had lost control of all its territory, including Gascony. Only one French town, Calais, was still run by the English, and the French won back this last English stronghold in the 1500s.

A deadly weapon
The longbow was the chief weapon of the English army. The archers could fire arrows so quickly from long range that they caused confusion and heavy casualties among mounted knights.

Besieging a town
Towns in France were besieged by both the French and English using early cannons. During this war, heavy firearms and gunpowder were used in Europe for the first time.

The Hundred Years War

During the war, the English defeated the French in battles such as Agincourt and Crécy through the skill of their longbowmen.

Because the English and French armies stripped the countryside of crops and cattle, many French peasants had to beg for food.

Later in the war the French were led by a farm girl, Joan of Arc. Joan led the French army to an important victory at Orléans.

The English captured Joan and, claiming she was a witch, burned her at the stake. But the French still went on to win battles and the war.

The Black Death

The Hundred Years War caused much suffering among ordinary people. But during the same period, an even more terrible event took place and affected countries in both Europe and Asia. It was known as the Black Death.

Bubonic plague was a disease that occurred throughout the world until the 18th century. It was carried by the fleas of plague-infected rats. The terrible outbreak of plague during the 1300s quickly spread from town to town, unhealthy places in those times when people threw their rubbish and waste matter into the streets. The plague also killed so many people in some country areas that complete villages disappeared forever. By the time the Black Death had subsided, it had killed more than 50 million people in Europe and millions more in Asia.

A European town during the Black Death

Towns with the plague were awful places to live in because as the disease spread, all normal life came to an end. Sometimes whole families died.

A strange procession

People would do anything to try to stop the plague. Some people even whipped themselves to show God how sorry they were for their past wrongs.

Burying the dead

A red cross on the door meant that the household had the plague. Carts came around at night to take the dead to huge unmarked death pits.

27

THE RENAISSANCE

During the 15th century, many people in Europe who could read and write began to take less notice of what their rulers and priests told them and to work out new ideas for themselves. They also became interested in the arts and learning about the ancient Greeks (*see pages 12-13*), and Romans (*see pages 14-17*). This new way of thinking, and rediscovery of earlier knowledge, led to an exciting period in history known as the Renaissance, a French word meaning "rebirth."

The Renaissance is remembered not only for the artistic and scientific achievements that were made during that time, but also for the changes that gradually occurred in the way people thought and lived. Although the Renaissance eventually spread all over Europe, it began in the cities of northern and central Italy.

The new wealthy merchants

When the Renaissance started, Italy was not a united country but was made up of different states. Some of the Italian states had become rich and powerful through buying and selling goods. The merchants from these states had sailed to eastern countries such as India and China and had brought back luxury goods such as spices and silks. By buying these goods at a low price and then selling them for high prices throughout Europe, merchants from city-states such as Florence, Venice, Genoa and Milan had become extremely rich.

The Medici

One of the most famous Renaissance families was the Medici family. The Medici had gained a large fortune through trade and banking, and the city of Florence was ruled by them for many years. But like many important Renaissance families, the Medici were not interested only in money and power. Rich men such as Cosimo and Lorenzo de' Medici also used their money and influence to help architects, artists, writers, and scholars.

An Italian city during the Renaissance

The picture on the right and the next two pages shows the capital city and surrounding countryside of an Italian city-state during the time of the Renaissance. A city-state was an independent city that controlled not only the land nearby but also less powerful cities and towns in the area.

Ruined castles

By this time the lands of former lords and rulers had been taken over by the city-states. The castles of these old estates were left empty.

Important buildings

Every merchant was a member of a guild, a group of people in the same trade who discussed business in a grand building called the guildhall. Another important building was the town hall where the city's government met.

Guildhall

Town hall

Main square

Grand palaces

Successful businessmen and merchants spent their money on magnificent houses and palaces. Only the most important citizens were allowed to build their homes in the city's main square.

Building and decorating

New buildings were constructed and decorated by masons and craftsmen who often copied the style of the buildings of ancient Greece and Rome.

Grand churches
As the city grew larger and its citizens more wealthy, a new cathedral was built to replace the original, smaller church.

Teachers and preachers
New schools and universities were built to educate the sons of wealthy citizens. The Church continued to be very powerful, but now there were more learned men about, writing and reading books, who were not priests. Some of these men began to question the Church's teachings.

Keeping the city's money
One of the city's most important businesses was banking. Each major city had its own bank, usually controlled by one powerful family.

Entrance to the city
The city had high walls and a closely-guarded main gate. The gate was closed every night and barricaded during wars with neighboring states. Just inside the main gate, monks looked after travelers and pilgrims in a specially built pilgrims' hospital.

Preacher

Pilgrims' hospital

Main gate

Chemist

Teacher

Clothmarket

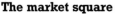

The market square
The busiest place in the city was the market square, which was always full of citizens buying or selling goods or discussing business. One of the state's most valuable products was wool, which was bought and sold in a special business place called a clothmarket.

Protecting the city
As the cities often quarreled with their neighbors, they paid *condottiere*, professional soldiers who recruited their own troops, to fight for them in time of war.

Hanging criminals
The city's gallows were placed in the market square so that the sight of executed criminals would act as a warning to the many passersby.

29

Life in the country

The countryside outside the city was controlled by the city-state. Most of the land was divided into farming estates owned by wealthy citizens. Some of the countryside also belonged to the Church. The peasants who worked on the estates led very hard lives. From dawn until dusk they were out in the fields tending crops and looking after animals.

Worshipping together

The one time that the rich and poor came together was at the local church where they all worshipped.

Country parties

The richest citizens built large country houses on their estates. On their country estates the landowners and their families could escape from plague, overcrowding, and summer heat.

Peasants' homes

Most peasants were able to rent a small piece of land from the landowners, on which they built a home and grew a few crops for their own use.

Peasant's cottage

Falconers

Artist

Prince

Vineyard

Entertainers

Entertaining visitors

The ruler of the city-state paid entertainers to perform before visitors from other countries and states.

The ruler's palace

The prince or ruler of a city-state was usually a member of a rich and powerful family. He was elected to rule only by the most important citizens in the state; the poor had no choice. Artists and scholars would be paid by the ruler to live and work in his palace.

Women in the Renaissance

Although girls in wealthy families were usually taught to read and write, women had less freedom than men. While very young, they were expected to marry a man chosen by their father. From then on, they stayed at home to run their household.

Good grazing land

During the winter months, shepherds drove flocks of sheep down from the hills to graze on lowland pasture. The pasture was usually badly-drained land near a river or the sea. The shepherds had to pay the city for the use of this land, but in return they were able to sell wool and lamb in the city's market.

Trading centers

As none of the Italian city-states was very far from the sea, it was easy for Italian merchants to travel from nearby ports to distant countries in search of trade. Some of the richer merchant families spent money on improving the Italian ports and merchant ships.

Port

Shepherds

Water mill

Olive grove

Mule train

Locally grown food

Among the locally grown foods were olives and grapes. People used the oil from the olives for cooking, while grapes from the vineyards were used to make wine.

Carrying goods

Many goods were carried to and from the city by mules because they were the best way of carrying food and materials for long distances over rough roads.

Renaissance art and architecture

The Medici and other rich people of the Renaissance used their money to encourage artistic people whose work gave them pleasure. Architects were paid to build grand palaces, churches, and bridges. Famous artists were asked to paint portraits or decorate the walls of houses and churches. Sculptors built statues to honor famous citizens.

The spread of knowledge

The Renaissance was also a time when people became more curious about the world they lived in. Rich men built libraries and universities, and with the invention of printing machines, books became more easily available, not only to priests and scholars but to ordinary people.

During the Renaissance, there were also brilliant men who were clever in several subjects. Leonardo da Vinci was not only a great painter, sculptor, and architect, he was also a brilliant engineer and scientist. Michelangelo was an equally outstanding sculptor, painter, architect, and poet.

The influence of the Renaissance

The many achievements that occurred in Italy at this time were soon heard and read about by people in other countries. By the end of the 16th century, many Renaissance ideas had spread to such places as France, Spain, Germany, and England. Scientists began to improve on the ideas of such men as the astronomer and mathematician Galileo, who constructed the first telescope to study the stars and planets.

Renaissance styles also influenced world architecture for many years. When Sir Christopher Wren planned St. Paul's Cathedral in London, he based his design on the great Renaissance cathedral of St. Peter's in Rome.

The city-states become less important

During the 16th century, explorers and traders from European countries such as Spain and England opened up new shipping routes for trade to Asia, Africa, and America. As these other European traders became increasingly successful, the merchants of the Italian city-states made less money and the cities themselves began to lose their importance and influence. But by this time, the achievements of their cleverest and most creative citizens had brought so many changes to the way that Europeans lived, that the Renaissance came to be known as the beginning of the modern age.

EXPLORERS AND ADVENTURERS

For most people living during the Renaissance (*see pages 28-31*) the world was a small place, stretching no farther than the nearest village or town. Many people believed that the world was flat and ships might sail too far and go over the edge.

But by the 1400s, merchants from the Italian city-states had brought back new kinds of luxury goods from Asia which became popular with rich people in Europe. Soon countries such as Portugal, Spain, and England were paying explorers to lead expeditions across the seas to look for new trading routes, so beginning the great age of European exploration.

While many explorers only wanted to find new trading routes, others became interested in claiming new territory that would bring their countries more power and wealth. Before long, explorers from Portugal, Spain, England, France, and Holland started settlements in parts of the world such as North and South America.

The great explorers were quickly followed by conquering armies and settlers. After the settlers came the slaves, millions of men and women herded together like animals on the most terrible of all trading routes. Starting with the Portuguese sailors who brought back African slaves to Europe in the 1400s, slavery lasted another 400 years before most countries abolished it.

Buying and selling slaves in Africa
The worst period of slavery since ancient times was between the 1400s and the 1800s, when European slave traders shipped at least 10 million Africans to work in the sugar, cotton, coffee, and tobacco plantations of North and South America and the West Indies.

Famous explorers

Vasco da Gama was a Portuguese explorer who made the first sea voyage from Europe to India by sailing around Africa. He later began settlements in India and Africa.

Christopher Columbus, an Italian, was given ships by the Spanish to discover new trade routes. Instead, he landed in the West Indies, encountering what was called the "New World."

Ferdinand Magellan sailed halfway around the world from Portugal, proving that the world was round and not flat. Magellan was killed before his long voyage ended.

Francis Drake was a pirate who often raided Spanish ships. He was also the first Englishman to sail around the world. After this voyage, Drake was knighted by Queen Elizabeth I.

The horrors of the slave trade

European or Arab slave traders would arrive at an African village and then force men and women to become slaves.

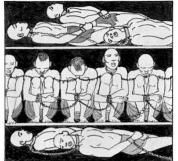

Slaves were taken to the African coast where hundreds would be packed together into each disease-ridden slave ship.

Slaves who survived the awful sea voyage and were not already bought were sold on the waterfront as soon as they came ashore.

Many slaves working on the European plantations died from overwork, disease, or the beatings they received from brutal overseers.

Trading human lives
Arab slave traders would travel inland to capture slaves. European traders would wait at the coast to buy the slaves and put them on ships.

Slave trade factories
For many years, Portugal was the main European country involved in the African slave trade. But when Portugal became less powerful, the British and Dutch began building slave trading forts along the African coast. Although they lived in far better conditions than the slaves, few Europeans could survive long in these forts, and the west coast of Africa became known as the "white man's grave."

Human chains
Groups of slaves often had to march hundreds of miles, linked together by iron collars and chains. Many died of disease before they reached the coast.

Waiting to be shipped
Slaves who survived the march to the coast were locked up in stockades and watched by armed guards until enough slaves had been collected to fill a ship.

THE ARMADA

By the 1580s, Spain had become the head of a huge empire and the most powerful country in the world (*see pages 32-33*). But despite Spain's strength, Spanish ships carrying gold, silver, and other treasure from the Americas were often attacked and robbed by English sailors such as Francis Drake (*see page 32*). English sailors were also encouraged by their queen, Elizabeth I, to raid Spanish settlements in Spain's American empire.

During this time Spain and England had also become enemies because of their different religious beliefs. While most English had become Protestants (*see below*), Spain remained a Catholic country. Finally, King Philip of Spain had had enough trouble with England. He became determined not only to destroy the English pirate ships but to invade England and make it a Catholic country once again. To do this, King Philip organized a great fleet of warships called the Armada (meaning "armed force") that the Spanish believed would be unbeatable.

But the Armada never reached England. Most of the Spanish ships were destroyed either by the English ships' guns or by terrible storms as they sailed around the British Isles. Spain's failure led to a weakening of its empire and to the growth of British power (*see pages 42-43*).

English and Spanish fighting ships

The Spanish Armada set out to invade England with 130 ships. But many of the ships were slow and had neither enough guns nor ammunition. The Spanish were also led by a commander with little experience of fighting at sea. The English navy had smaller, faster ships that were not only better designed and equipped but were commanded by experienced seamen.

The English flagship

The *Ark Royal* was the English commander's flagship during the battle with the Spanish Armada. Originally built for exploring new lands, the *Ark Royal* was a fast-moving, well-defended ship with three gun decks.

Defeating the Armada

The English set fire ships packed with gunpowder toward the Armada and then fired on the fleeing ships.

Religious wars in Europe

During the 1500s, some Europeans began to follow the beliefs of Martin Luther, a German priest who disagreed with certain teachings of the Catholic Church. Luther eventually started a new branch of Christianity called Protestantism. Soon Catholics and Protestants were fighting one another in a series of cruel and bloody wars that divided Europe.

English commander   English seaman   Spanish soldier   Spanish commander

New faster warships

By the time of the Spanish Armada, the English had designed a new type of warship that had fewer masts and decks, making them faster than warships used by other countries. The English ships also carried heavy new guns that could hit an enemy ship from a greater distance than the guns of the Spanish ships.

Spanish galleons

Galleons were large warships, used by navies from the 1500s to the 1800s. Spanish galleons were designed to bring back treasure from new lands and were slower and more difficult to sail than English galleons. The bottom of the ship was weighed down with ballast, heavy material such as stone or lead that kept the ship steady.

Soldiers and sailors (*left*)

Because the Spanish were expecting to invade England, there were thousands more soldiers on board the Armada fleet than there were sailors. The English, on the other hand, had 14,000 sailors and only 1,500 soldiers on board their ships. As the battle between the two sides was fought only at sea, the English benefited from having more sailors than soldiers.

Gun deck

Gun deck

Ship's stores

Ballast

Cargo in the Spanish ships

The Spanish ships were made heavier and slower by having their lower decks crammed full of stores needed for the invasion of England. The cargo included food, weapons, and horses.

35

CONQUEST OF THE NEW WORLD

Only a hundred years after the European encounter with the Americas (*see pages 32-33*), people from all over Europe began to sail across the Atlantic Ocean to the "New World." Some Europeans came as settlers hoping to find a better life, while others were soldiers and adventurers trying to get rich as quickly as possible. It was these two very different groups of people who conquered the "New World."

The first Europeans to journey through South and Central America were mainly Portuguese and Spanish soldiers. The Portuguese took over the part of South America that is now the country of Brazil. Here many Portuguese became rich by running plantations that sent sugar, cotton, and tobacco back to Europe. The Spanish *conquistadores* (meaning "conquerors") also made Spain rich by taking silver from Peru and gold from Mexico. Both Portugal and Spain were to build up large empires based on their New World conquests.

Some of the Europeans who came to North America were also adventurers or traders, but most were settlers who wanted to live better lives in a new land. Although many of these early settlers were farmers, merchants, and craftsmen from countries such as Germany, France, Sweden, and Holland, it was the English who founded the largest settlements on the east coast of America. During the 1600s and the 1700s, these English settlements grew into towns and then into 13 colonies. It was these 13 New England colonies that became the first 13 states of the United States of America (*see pages 44-45*).

A Puritan settlement in New England

The Puritans who founded the first New England settlements modeled their buildings on those in the villages they had left behind in England. But they had to add an enclosing stockade to keep out unfriendly intruders.

Keeping guard

Puritan settlers often used force to take and keep American Indian lands.

Inhabitants of New England

The first English settlers in America included many craftsmen and farmers looking for work or new land. Some settlers also wanted freedom to practice their religious beliefs. This group included the Pilgrims, a group of Puritans who started the settlement of Plymouth. The Indians, as the settlers called the original inhabitants of America, often tried to stop the settlers from taking their lands.

American Indian

Pilgrim

Farmer

Housewife and daughter

Settlement storehouse
The building holding supplies was so important that men guarded it from a nearby watchtower.

Near woods and water
The settlers needed wood to build homes and furniture, and water for drinking, washing, and fishing.

Houses of local wood
The large areas of forest in New England made wood the most popular building material.

Watching the settlers
Although some local Indians were friendly, others attacked settlers who took Indian lands.

The conquistadores

Among the conquistadores, Spanish conquerors of South and Central America, was Hernán Cortés, who defeated the Aztec rulers of Mexico.

During an Aztec revolt against the Spanish, the Aztec emperor was killed. The Spanish then destroyed the Aztec civilization.

With fewer than 200 men, another conquistador, Francisco Pizarro, discovered and conquered the Inca Empire in Peru.

Although the Inca ruler promised Pizarro a roomful of gold, the Inca people were killed and their cities were looted and burned.

RICH AND POOR IN THE 1600s

The great age of European exploration (*see pages 32-33*) brought power and wealth to many European merchants and businessmen. Among the richest merchants in Europe were the Dutch. They made their wealth from owning ships that brought back spices, cotton, silk, and slaves from trading forts in America, Asia, and Africa. Indeed, between about 1600 and 1700, Holland was the world's leading trading power and sea power.

With their newfound wealth, the Dutch merchants built large new houses that they filled with beautiful paintings and furniture. For rich Europeans, the 1600s were a time of great success and luxury.

But the 1600s were not good times for the poor of Europe. Few poor people benefited from the new trading wealth. Every country in Europe had thousands of people who could find no work and who had to beg and steal in order to survive. By the end of the 1600s, the gap between rich and poor was wider than ever before.

A peasant's home

Even when a country such as Holland became wealthy from overseas trade, the majority of its people were still poor. Dutch peasants were rarely short of food, but they could afford only the simplest furniture and plainest clothing. Some peasants were too poor to own a farmhouse and had to live in a small hut (*below*).

A wealthy merchant's house

During the 1600s, many Europeans who made money from business and trade lived extremely comfortably. This Dutch merchant's house (below) is a good example of how wealthy Europeans lived.

Beautiful furnishings

As businessmen and merchants made more money, they showed it off by buying grander furniture, paintings, and more expensive decorations.

Keeping servants

All but the poorest families had at least one servant. A servant was needed to prepare and serve the large meals, while other servants might be employed to do the washing, cleaning, shopping, or to help the lady of the house.

The outside of the house

The houses of wealthier Europeans began to be built of brick instead of wood. These fine houses with decorated entrances and large windows must have amazed poor passersby, who often lived in dark, overcrowded rooms.

The different floors
The merchant's family lived on the ground floor and first floor of the house. Above the family's bedrooms were storerooms and servants' bedrooms.

New discoveries in medicine

Little was known about curing illnesses until the 1880s. The cure for injured arms or legs was to cut them off.

In the 1700s a doctor, William Harvey, discovered that blood is pumped around the body by the heart.

A Dutchman, Anton van Leeuwenhoek, made scientific discoveries about blood through early microscopes.

In the 1800s, Edward Jenner's discovery of vaccination led to the prevention of many diseases.

The first public theaters in England
Until public theaters such as the Globe in London (*right*) were built in the 1500s, plays had only been put on in schools or rich people's homes, or by bands of actors touring the countryside. In the public theaters, anybody could watch plays by such writers as the great English playwright William Shakespeare.

Going to the theater
The best seats in the theater were in the balconies that surrounded the stage. Other people could sit or stand in the area in front of the stage known as the yard. As there were no electric lights, plays had to start in the afternoon and end before dark.

William Shakespeare

Stage

Balconies

Yard

Servants' quarters
Servants spent their days in the kitchen and other rooms in the basement of the house. At night, they slept in rooms under the roof.

Male actors only
Until the 1660s, no women were allowed on the stage, and all the women's roles were played by boys. The theaters of this time had no curtains, there was little scenery, and actors rarely changed their costumes.

KINGS AND COMMONERS

During the 1600s, powerful European countries such as Spain, Austria, France, and England often quarreled with each other. This made their kings and queens important people as it was they who made the major decisions that affected their countries.

England was made weaker by having a civil war between the followers of King Charles I and his Parliament. Charles lost the war and was executed. However, countries with strong leaders such as Louis XIV of France and Peter the Great of Russia became more powerful. But even while Louis XIV was becoming more important in Europe, his wars and constant waste of money made life harder for the "commoners", the people who made up most of the population of France.

The most important courtiers
Even though they had no say in how the king governed France, only the richest and most powerful men were allowed to wait upon the king and queen. These top courtiers held such positions as Grand Master of the King's Household and Master of the King's Robes.

Europe's greatest palace
When Louis XIV was at his most powerful, he decided to build a magnificent palace at Versailles where he and his household, court, and government could be seen living in splendor (*see below*). The largest palace in Europe, Versailles is surrounded by beautiful gardens with lakes, fountains, and statues.

The power of the Sun King
Because he was so powerful and had such a magnificent court, King Louis XIV of France was often called the Sun King. Louis had total control over the government of France and the lives of his people, including the 25,000 who lived in his palace at Versailles.

Ladies of the court
Most of the fashionable ladies of the court were either the wives or daughters of important men, or attendants and companions to the queen and her daughters.

The best musicians
The court of Louis XIV attracted the best writers, artists, and musicians. Special music was composed for the many court performances.

Brilliant craftsmen
Many top designers, craftsmen, and architects lived at the palace with their families. They were employed to keep the palace and its grounds in good condition.

Architect and wife

Musicians

Grand Master of the Household

Ladies of the court

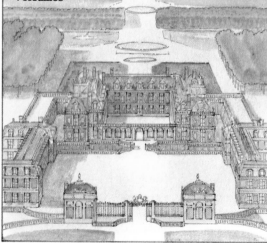

Versailles

Royal family

Louis XIV

The royal family
At the center of life at the French court were Louis XIV, his queen, and his children. Louis believed that as the members of the royal family were the most important people in France, they should be on view to the public from the time they were dressed in the morning until they went to bed.

The poorest people

Most of the people ruled by the king were laborers and peasants. They had much harder lives than people working at the Palace of Versailles.

Palace staff

Large numbers of cleaners, gardeners, coach drivers, cooks, and other servants kept the palace running smoothly.

Peasants

Palace staff

Naval officer   Admiral   General

Members of the army and navy

Although only naval commanders and army generals were important members of the court, 8,000 soldiers from the best French regiments were stationed at Versailles to guard the king.

Peter the Great of Russia

During the 1600s, Russia was a poor, backward country ruled by an all-powerful emperor, or czar, his nobles, and the Church. Most Russians were poor peasants who had little freedom.

Then one of Russia's strongest rulers, Peter the Great, made his country into a world power by building a powerful navy and by forcing the Russians to copy the European way of life.

Palace at St. Petersburg

Russian gold coins

Russian nobility

Peter the Great

Russian serfs

Peter leading his army

Ships of the Russian navy

The English Civil War

King Charles I quarreled often with the English Parliament. Finally, the king went to Parliament to arrest parliamentary leaders who opposed him.

Soon after, war broke out in England between those who supported Parliament and King Charles' army. After several big battles, the king's side lost the war.

After the war, the king was accused by Parliament of betraying England. King Charles was found guilty at his trial and had his head cut off in public.

The parliamentary leader, Oliver Cromwell, then ruled England. The dead king's son, Charles, escaped to France but became king after Cromwell's death.

41

THE BRITISH EMPIRE

As islanders living off the mainland of Europe, the British have always been great traders and explorers. And of all the European countries that started overseas settlements in the 1600s (*see pages 32-33 and 36-37*), it was the people from the British Isles – England, Scotland, Ireland, and Wales – who were to establish the largest empire of all time. By the 1900s, the British Empire included a quarter of the world's people and land.

In the 1600s and 1700s, the empire included the American colonies in New England (*see pages 36-37*) and territories in Canada won from the French. But the American colonies were lost during the American Revolution (*see pages 44-45*).

After the 1700s, the British Empire was made up of countries taken over by the British in Asia and Africa, and lands encountered by explorers such as James Cook. These countries did not win their independence until after World War II (*see pages 60-61*). Many of them joined the Commonwealth of Nations as equal partners of Britain.

A great explorer
James Cook was the greatest of all the British explorers whose journeys helped expand the British Empire. Among the places he explored were Hawaii and the coasts of New Zealand and eastern Australia.

The British in India
In the 1600s, the British East India Company built trading posts in India. By the 1850s, Britain had become the leading power in India, and British officials often attended important Indian ceremonies (below).

Cook became famous when the maps he made of the St. Lawrence River in Canada helped the British capture the city of Quebec from the French (*left*). This success gave him the chance to lead a British naval expedition to the Pacific island of Tahiti (*above*). During the three voyages he made in the 1760s and 1770s, Cook claimed the Australian coast for Britain and made friends with Maoris in New Zealand (*above*). On his last voyage, he landed on Vancouver Island. He was later killed on the Pacific island of Hawaii.

Top-hatted officials
The British in the procession were officials of the East India Company. They can be easily picked out by their top hats.

Homage to an emperor
The procession mainly consists of Indian princes and their followers who are paying homage to an Indian ruler.

The length of British rule
England's Queen Victoria became empress of India in 1876. Until the 1940s, India was ruled by British government officials or by Indian rulers who agreed to support the British.

The real power in India
By the time this procession took place, the Indian emperor being honored had no real power. Most of India was run by the East India Company and controlled by British-led forces.

AN AGE OF REVOLUTION

The American Revolution and the French Revolution were two of the most important events of all time. The American Revolution began because many people there were dissatisfied with British rule and wanted freedom to govern themselves. A similar situation occurred in France 14 years later.

By the middle of the 1700s, the 13 British colonies in America (*see pages 36-37*) were used to looking after themselves and no longer wanted to be governed by a British Parliament thousands of miles away. When the British sent troops to America to try to seize the colonists' weapons and ammunition, the colonists rebelled against their rulers. In 1775, fighting broke out between the colonists and British troops, and the following year the rebels issued the Declaration of Independence.

Eight years of fighting ended when colonists defeated the British, and their country became recognized as a new nation, the United States of America.

After the Civil War in England (*see pages 40-41*), the English monarch had very little power, and important decisions were made by the British Parliament. But across the English Channel in France, there was no formal parliament, and all the wealth and power was controlled by the French king, his nobles, and the Church. By the late 1700s, most ordinary French people wished they could be ruled more fairly and were dissatisfied with their poverty.

Finally, in 1789, heavy taxes, food shortages, and bad government by the king, Louis XVI, and his ministers led to a revolution. There then followed 10 years of violent struggle, during which the French monarchy was overthrown and a new system of government set up. Although the French Revolution caused many innocent people to lose their lives, it introduced many important ideas, especially the right of all human beings to be treated equally under the law.

The American Revolution

When the revolutionary war broke out in 1775, the British had a full-time army already in America that included foreign troops called Hessians. The British also had the support of many Indian nations. The colonists' army was made up of volunteers, including "minutemen," so called because they were ready to fight "at a minute's notice." Later in the war, the colonists were helped by Britain's European enemies, France, Spain, and Holland. With so many enemies, the British were always outnumbered in the war.

Minuteman | Officer in the American army | Militiaman | Hessian soldier | Officer and private in the British army

Among the events before the war between Britain and the colonists was the Boston Massacre, when British soldiers fired into a crowd, killing five people.

Colonial anger at having to pay tax on tea from Britain led to the Boston Tea Party, where some colonists threw tea from British ships into Boston Harbor.

At Christmas, 1776, the colonies' commander in the war, George Washington, crossed the Delaware River to defeat the British at the Battle of Trenton.

The British army was finally beaten by Washington at the Battle of Yorktown. Two years later, the British agreed to American independence.

Death on the guillotine

During the French Revolution, thousands of men and women lost their lives. Many of them had their heads cut off in public by an instrument called the guillotine. Among the guillotine's victims were Louis XVI and his wife and, when they became unpopular, men who had started the revolution.

An instrument of death

The executioner worked the guillotine by releasing a heavy iron knife so that it fell between two posts on to the victim's neck. Nobles, priests, and other "enemies" of the revolution were taken in carts to where the guillotine stood in a large square. Here the executions were watched by many people who supported the revolution.

The end of the "Terror"

After a terrible time called the "Reign of Terror" when many people were executed every day, the most violent leaders of the revolution were put to death in their turn.

A humane killer

Strangely enough, the guillotine was at first seen as a humane form of execution, because it gave its victims a faster, less painful death than most other forms of punishment.

Taking away the bodies

After an execution, the victim's head and body were quickly taken away in baskets and buried in unmarked mass graves.

NAPOLEON BONAPARTE

Few men or women have dominated the age they lived in as did Napoleon Bonaparte, the French emperor who was also one of the greatest soldier-conquerors of all time.

After the breakdown of law and order during the French Revolution (*see pages 44-45*), the French people were happy to have a single strong ruler. Napoleon had become a great hero in France because of his brilliant leadership of a French army that defeated the Austrians in Italy. Within two years of this victory, Napoleon had seized power from the government that was formed after the revolution.

As ruler of France, Napoleon not only improved the schools and universities, but he also set up the first Bank of France and made many lasting changes to French law. Above all, he made France the chief power in Europe. From the time Napoleon became emperor of France in 1804 until his final defeat at the Battle of Waterloo in 1815, it was only the British navy's command of the seas that prevented Napoleon from controlling the whole of western Europe.

Symbols of glory
Napoleon owed his success to his brilliance as a soldier and the greatness of his army. Regiments in Napoleon's army proudly carried his name on their flags (*right*). Napoleon's personal emblem was the eagle, used earlier by the army of the Roman Empire.

1 Napoleon was born on the island of Corsica. He became a lieutenant in the French army at the age of 16. During the French Revolution, Napoleon's troops defended the revolutionary government from angry mobs (*above*).

2 Napoleon was soon made a commander in the French army. After several illustrious victories, he crowned himself and his wife, Josephine (*above*), as emperor and empress of the French.

3 The French army (*above*) was devoted to Napoleon and always fought bravely under his command. As countries such as Austria and Spain were defeated, most of Europe came under Napoleon's control.

4 But just when he was at his most powerful, Napoleon made the terrible mistake of invading Russia. He lost most of his army when he had to retreat to France during the freezing Russian winter (*above*).

Regimental flag in
Napoleon's time

Napoleon's personal
emblem

New European nations
During the 1860s,
Giuseppe Garibaldi
(pictured in the
carriage) and his
volunteer army of "red
shirts" helped unify the
many small states of
Italy into one country.
The German states
also began to unite,
under the leadership
of Otto von Bismarck,
chancellor of Prussia.

5 Several European countries then joined together and
defeated Napoleon, who was forced to give up his
crown. But Napoleon soon raised a new army which was
beaten by the British and their allies at Waterloo (*above*).

A great leader
One of the most
famous paintings
of Napoleon
shows him leading
his army on a march
across the mountains
from France into Italy,
where he defeated
the Austrians
at Marengo.

6 Napoleon then became a prisoner of war and was
sent to the lonely British island of St. Helena (*above*).
The man who had once ruled over most of Europe was
still guarded by British troops when he died.

47

THE INDUSTRIAL REVOLUTION

In about the middle of the 18th century, there were changes in the way people in Britain worked and lived. Most of the changes were brought about by the invention of machines that could produce goods more quickly than could people working with their hands. We now call this period of time the Industrial Revolution.

Spinning and weaving machines

The first machines to bring great changes were designed to make it both easier and faster for people to spin cotton and weave cloth. The new machines were first driven by water power and later by another new invention, the steam engine. As steam engines needed fuel to make them work, most of the factories or mills that used the new machines were built near coalfields. New towns grew up around the factories, and the British cotton industry became the most important in the world.

Coal and iron

During the Industrial Revolution, coal became extremely important, not only because it was needed to drive the new steam engines, but because it was used in making iron and steel. These two metals were used for machinery, tools, water pipes, bridges and, later, ships and railroad lines. Another new invention called the blast furnace made it easier to produce iron and steel in bigger quantities.

Changes in farming

New inventions and types of machines also helped farmers grow and harvest crops more easily. These included new types of plows and seed drills. During this time, farmers also developed better types of farm animals, such as sheep with more wool and cows that produced more milk.

Country and town life in England during the Industrial Revolution

The pictures on the right and the next two pages show how many people's lives changed during the Industrial Revolution. New towns grew up around important factories. New mines, buildings, and canals were built near farming land. On the newly enlarged farms, new machines helped the farmer produce more food.

Bigger and better farms
Many country people lost their jobs and land at this time. Landowners wanted their farms to be bigger in order to produce more food. So they refused to rent land to poorer farmers, who then lost their living. The extra crops grown on the bigger farms helped feed people in the new towns.

Wind power
Despite the new steam power, wind power was still used to work windmills, machines that were used either to pump water or to grind corn.

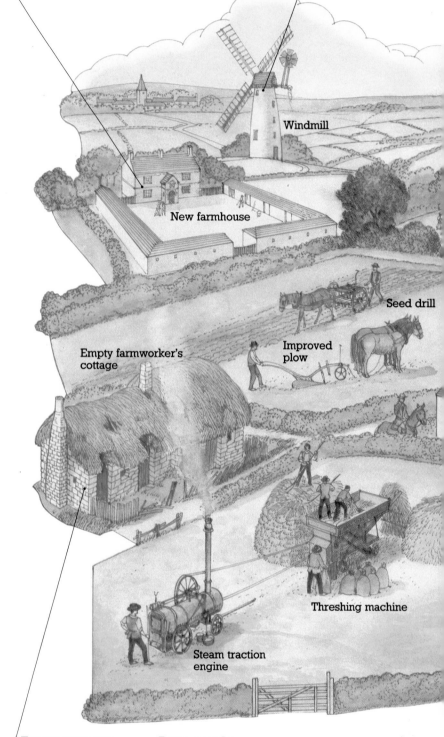

Windmill

New farmhouse

Seed drill

Empty farmworker's cottage

Improved plow

Threshing machine

Steam traction engine

Empty cottages
With less work on the farms, many farmworkers had to leave their homes and look for work in the new towns.

Better roads
People paid to use the new hard-surfaced roads at a tollhouse by the roadside. The money paid for more new roads.

Places to stay
Travelers who came from the country to the new towns could find food or a bed for the night at an inn.

New farm machinery
Many new inventions helped farmers. New types of plows and other machines helped make the planting and harvesting of crops much easier.

Coal and iron mines
The invention of the steam engine meant a greater need for coal. Another invention, the blast furnace, made it easier to produce iron and steel. Big new coal mines and ironworks were opened up, and more people began working in these "heavy" industries.

Making beer
Steam engines were put into breweries, the places where beer was made. Machines meant that more beer could be produced more easily.

Storing the town's food
Railroads and barges brought food into the new towns. The food was stored in warehouses built near the places where the food was unloaded by the barges.

Coal mine

Iron mine

Hay rake

Reaper

Tollhouse

Sail reaper

Brewery

Warehouses

Inn

Towpath

Man-made rivers
New waterways were built so that goods could be easily taken from town to town. Barges loaded with goods were pulled by horses along special tracks called towpaths.

Faster sea journeys
The new steam-powered ships meant the end of the great days of sailing ships.

New types of bridges
Bridges began to be built with iron. Giant suspension bridges hung from heavy iron chains could cross great distances. Viaduct bridges were built with arches and carried roads or trains across town centers. Special bridges were also built to cross canals.

Suspension bridge

Coal train

Iron bridge

Machine-making factory

Pottery

Viaduct

The coming of the railroads
Trains were found to be so useful that within a few years of the first steam locomotives, all the main towns in England were linked by railroad.

Passenger trains
Used at first for carrying coal from mines, trains were soon used for passenger travel.

Poor housing
Factory workers often lived in badly built, overcrowded houses with no water supply.

More shopping areas
As the towns grew bigger, people wanted to buy food and other goods nearby, and not just from one big central marketplace. Many new shops were built, and some of the larger ones became the first department stores.

Away from the smoke
People who owned shops and factories or who had special skills, such as doctors and lawyers, often built new houses away from the center of town.

New shops

Steam-powered cotton mill

The coming of the railroads
Before the Industrial Revolution, most goods were transported by horses or wagons on bad roads or muddy tracks. But with the building of new factories and bigger towns came the need for better types of transportation to take goods from the country to the town and from one town to another. The first solution was to build better roads with hard surfaces and special inland waterways called canals. But these kinds of transportation were soon overtaken by the building of steam locomotives and railroads.

Of all the developments of the Industrial Revolution, the building of the railroads was probably the most important. For the railroads were not only a cheap and easy way of taking factory-made goods to where they could be sold, they also made it easier for people to travel from place to place.

Living in the new towns
Another way that the Industrial Revolution changed people's lives was that most people no longer lived in the country but in factory towns built near coalfields.

Some people, such as landowners, factory owners, businessmen, and shopkeepers, made a lot of money from the new factories and goods. But most of the people who lived in the towns were factory workers. Even when they had jobs, they had little money and lived in poorly built, overcrowded houses. In order to pay their rent and get food, whole families, even children, had to work very long hours each day. Sunday was the only day off.

The spread of the Industrial Revolution
Soon other countries such as Germany, France, and the United States had their own Industrial Revolutions. These countries often improved the new machines or developed their own inventions.

Most people who were alive during the Industrial Revolution would not have known much about the new inventions and machines. But they would have been aware that their everyday lives were changing in many ways. They could see that many people were going to live and work in the new towns instead of in the country. They could also see that many goods, including types of food and clothing, were becoming cheaper and easier to buy.

Although the Industrial Revolution created problems for the growing towns and cities, it also brought a better way of life for millions of people.

Factories in the new towns
All the new towns were built up around factories. These might be potteries for making china, mills for producing cotton or wool, or factories for making machinery and tools.

Working in factories
Factory workers, including women and children, worked long hours operating and cleaning machines.

THE FRONTIER MOVES WEST

When the American colonies became the United States of America (*see pages 44-45*), most of the new country's citizens lived on its eastern coast. But as more and more people arrived from Europe, pressure grew for Americans to start pushing their frontier farther westward. Traders and explorers told of rich farmlands and great forests, and soon the trickle of pioneers traveling west became a flood.

After long and dangerous journeys, the pioneers had to build homes and clear and plow land. Only then could they start permanent communities with stores, churches, and schools. From these small settlements grew the towns and cities that have made the U.S. the most powerful industrial nation in the world.

One major disruption of American progress was the terrible civil war that broke out in 1861 between the slaveowning South and the non-slaveowning North. The main results of the war were the abolition of slavery in the U.S. and the final union of the southern and northern American states.

Pioneer supplies
As they were riding into a vast wilderness, the pioneers packed their wagons full of vital supplies such as farming and household tools, flour, seeds, fruit trees, and a plow. They also took furniture and livestock.

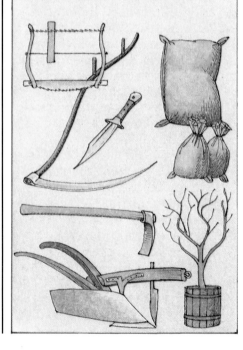

A wagon train traveling westward
The pioneers pushed the American frontier westward in two separate waves. From the 1760s, the first wave pushed inland from the East Coast to beyond the Mississippi River. In the 1840s, a second wave took the pioneers on journeys of several months to Oregon or California on the West Coast.

A welcome stop
Early traders and, later, the American army set up trading posts or forts in wild country. These places were reached with gratitude by the travel-weary pioneers.

Water bucket

Brake blocks

Pioneer transportation
Although some pioneers traveled west in ordinary farm wagons, the best form of transportation was a wagon called a prairie schooner, pulled by teams of oxen or mules.

A long-distance home
The prairie schooner had a canvas roof to keep out rain and sun. Its wheels had wide rims to prevent them from sticking in mud. The inside of the wagon was usually so full of belongings that the family had to sleep and eat outside.

American Civil War

The Civil War was the first modern war, bringing death and destruction not only to the two opposing armies, but also to American civilians.

Both the North (the Union) and South (the Confederacy) used new types of weapons, including mines, repeating rifles, and iron-clad ships.

After the Confederacy was defeated, President Abraham Lincoln, leader of the Union, was shot dead by a sympathizer of the South.

Confederate soldier

Union soldier

Wagon trains
Many families usually made up a wagon train so that they could share supplies and help each other.

A Plains Indian's home
The Indian nations of the grassland areas of America spent their lives following the buffalo herds. Buffalo meat was their main food, and they used the skins to make their tepees. Sometimes in winter, friendly American Indians camped near forts in order to get food.

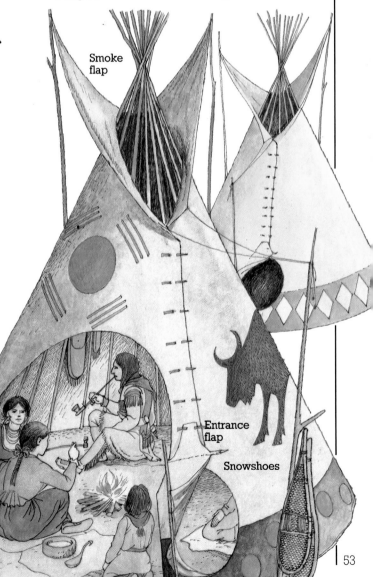

Smoke flap

Toolbox

Entrance flap

Snowshoes

Disaster strikes!
At any time illness, food shortages, or a broken wagon wheel could delay the pioneers' journey.

Under attack
American Indians often attacked the pioneers because they took Indian land and killed the buffalo.

53

DIGGING FOR GOLD

Since ancient times, no metal has been more sought after than gold. In order to find gold, people have traveled many miles, faced terrible hardships, and killed each other.

During the 19th century, the discovery of gold in the United States, Canada, South Africa, and Australia caused thousands of prospectors to rush to the goldfields. Within months, new towns had sprung up and a few lucky miners had made fortunes. For most of the miners, however, their back-breaking work only brought them disappointment.

The first great American gold rush occurred in California in the 1840s. Later, gold was also found in Colorado and the Klondike area of Canada. In the 1850s, so many prospectors went to the Australian gold rush and stayed on in their new country that between the years 1850 and 1860, the number of people living in Australia more than doubled.

Bushranger attacks
Miners found that they could get a better price for their gold in a town rather than at the diggings. But the journey to town could be dangerous, because armed criminals called bushrangers often lay in ambush. Bushrangers were usually escaped convicts who lived in unsettled areas called the bush.

The first Australians
The diggers often treated the Aborigines, the original inhabitants of Australia, badly by beating them or taking away their lands.

Paying to dig
Diggers had to buy a gold-mining license. The money paid for police in the goldfields.

A plot to mine
The authorities gave each licensed miner the same size plot of land in the diggings.

Bushranger

An Australian gold-mining camp
For the thousands of prospectors who worked from dawn until dusk in the Australian goldfields or "diggings," life was hard. Food was scarce and expensive, there were no hospitals, and many diggers went armed in case they were attacked and robbed.

Diggers' families
Although life was hard for the miners' families in their huts and tents, most helped with the daily digging.

The Klondike gold rush

One of the world's biggest gold rushes took place in the freezing Klondike region of northwest Canada. After gold was first discovered there in 1896, thousands of prospectors made the long and difficult journey to the mining camps that sprang up around Dawson City, the only town of the Klondike goldfield.

Types of gold

Dust

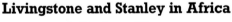

Flakes

Nuggets

Gold is found either as dust or flakes on riverbeds or as pieces called nuggets that are embedded in rocks.

A terrible journey

To reach the goldfield, prospectors either had to make a long river trip or climb a high mountain pass. Many turned back or died from hunger or cold.

Essential supplies

On their way over the mountains, prospectors had to pick up enough supplies to last them for a year's trip.

Livingstone and Stanley in Africa

Until the 1800s, no European had traveled far inland from the coast of Africa. Then in the 1840s a Scot, David Livingstone (*above*), traveled deep into the interior of Africa to convert Africans to Christianity.

After years of exploring Africa, Livingstone became "lost." A journalist, Henry Morton Stanley, set out to look for the great explorer. When Stanley finally found Livingstone, the story made Stanley world famous.

After Livingstone's death, Stanley carried on the older man's work in Africa. Stanley led several expeditions to explore the continent, including a dangerous trip along the length of the Congo River (*above*).

55

WORLD WAR I

The war of 1914-1918 comes second only to World War II (*see pages 60-61*) as the most destructive of all time.

War broke out in 1914 because of trading and territorial rivalries between the Allied Powers (who included Britain, France, Russia and, later, the United States of America) and the Central Powers (Germany, Austria-Hungary and Turkey). When, after a few months, it became clear that neither side could win a quick victory, each army constructed a defense network of trenches that eventually stretched right across Western Europe. For the rest of the war, great armies faced each other across a devastated no-man's-land. In four years of fighting, there were no decisive battles, little territory was gained or lost, and yet an estimated 10 million men died from bullets, shell-fire, or disease.

Crossing no-man's-land
Night patrols had to go on nerve-racking trips across no-man's-land to recover their dead or wounded or to check enemy movements.

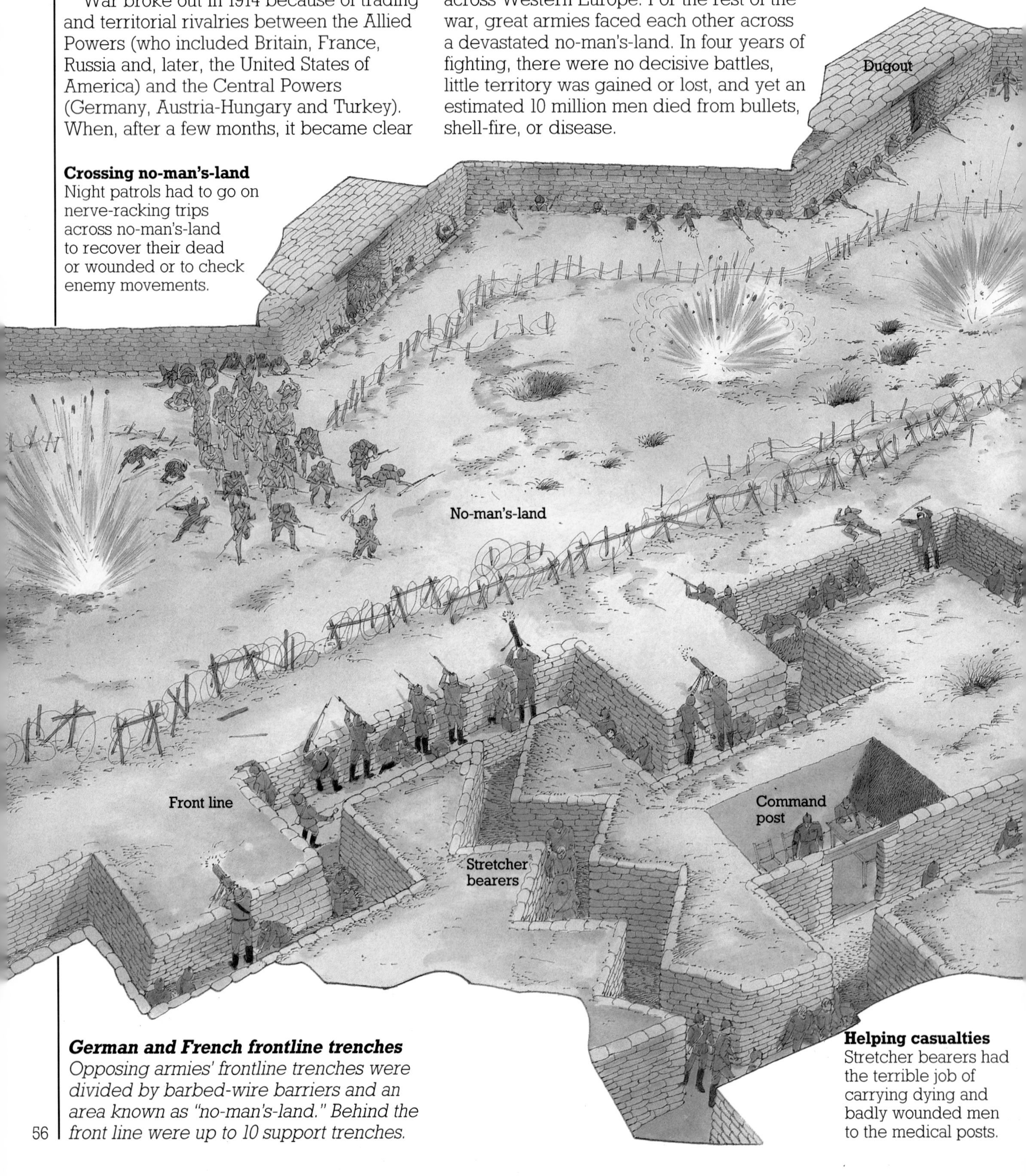

Dugout

No-man's-land

Front line

Stretcher
bearers

Command
post

German and French frontline trenches
Opposing armies' frontline trenches were divided by barbed-wire barriers and an area known as "no-man's-land." Behind the front line were up to 10 support trenches.

Helping casualties
Stretcher bearers had the terrible job of carrying dying and badly wounded men to the medical posts.

The only shelter

An important part of any frontline trench was the dugout, a shelter for soldiers from enemy gunfire and bad weather.

The armed forces

During the war, Allied troops totaled 48 million, of whom 5 million died. The Central Powers, with less than 26 million troops, lost at least 3.5 million lives. A further 21 million troops were wounded. The biggest losses were suffered by France, Russia, Germany, and Austria-Hungary.

British Vickers machine gun

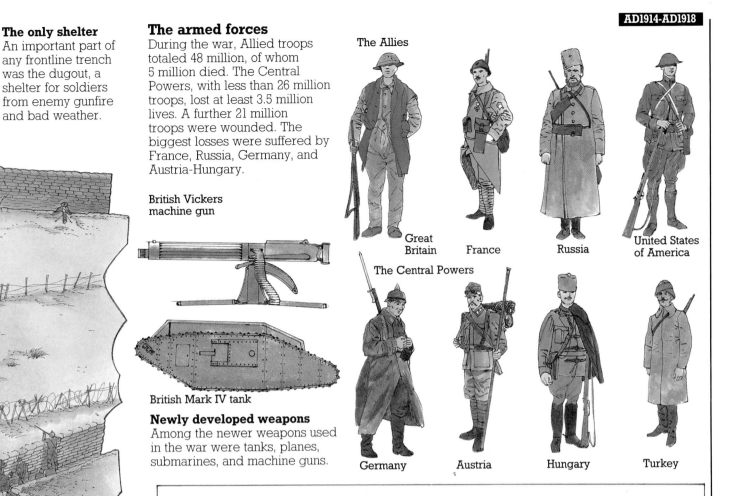

The Allies

Great Britain

France

Russia

United States of America

British Mark IV tank

Newly developed weapons

Among the newer weapons used in the war were tanks, planes, submarines, and machine guns.

The Central Powers

Germany

Austria

Hungary

Turkey

The Russian Revolution

In the early 1900s, Russia was a poor country ruled by a czar. Poverty and hardship led many Russians to support revolutionaries such as Lenin, whose Bolshevik party wished to overthrow the czar. Toward the end of World War I, the Bolsheviks seized power. The czar was forced to abdicate and was later executed. As Russia's new ruler, Lenin then made peace with Germany and set up the world's first communist state.

During World War I, there were riots as people blamed the czar and his advisers for Russian defeats.

Rasputin, the czar's most hated adviser, was murdered because of his influence over the czar and his wife.

Although their officers tried to stop them, many Russian soldiers began to desert from the front line.

The czar abdicated, and Lenin called on discontented soldiers to help seize power from the government.

The Bolsheviks eventually defeated the government troops and gained control of Russia's major cities.

Bitter fighting followed the revolution. Many starving people had to beg for food in the streets of cities.

Support trenches

Connected to the front line by communication trenches, support trenches held stores, medical aid posts, and command posts.

LIFE IN THE MODERN AGE

Although people who lived in earlier centuries had seen periods of important change such as the Renaissance (*see pages 28-31*) and the Industrial Revolution (*see pages 48-51*), no other century in history has seen so many changes happen so quickly as the 20th century. Some of these changes were brought about by World War I (*see pages 56-57*) and World War II (*see pages 60-61*), but most of the changes came in peacetime through scientific developments.

It is easier to realize how quickly the world has changed during the 20th century if you remember that in the year 1900 no person had ever watched television, listened to the radio, kept food cool in a refrigerator, or flown in an airplane, and that very few people had ridden in a car, seen a moving picture, or spoken to someone else on the telephone.

Most important of all, the 20th century saw such great developments in caring for people's health that a person who lived in the wealthy countries of Europe or in the United States and who might expect to live 50 years in 1900, could expect to live more than 70 years in the 1990s.

Developments that changed people's lives

Few centuries have brought as many changes to ordinary people's lives as the 20th century. Developments in transportation, communications, medicine, and the mass production of many goods have made wealthier parts of the world healthier and pleasanter places to live in.

Taking to the air

In 1903, two American brothers, Orville and Wilbur Wright, made the first powered flight in a craft which was heavier than air (*above*). As the 20th century progressed, airplanes became the most popular way for people to travel long distances. They also became important weapons in wartime.

Luxury sea voyages

Passenger ships and warships became larger than ever, and many people enjoyed sailing between America and Europe in floating "hotels" such as the liner *Queen Elizabeth* (*left*).

Taking pictures

Although the first photographs were taken in the 1820s, photography became a popular hobby in the 1900s with the improvement of both cameras (*right*) and types of film.

New inventions in the home

Once electricity began to be introduced into people's homes in the early 1900s, many families benefited from this new system of lighting that eventually replaced gas and candles. Electricity also meant the development of home appliances such as the iron, washing machine, vacuum cleaner, and refrigerator (*far right*). Among new forms of communication, the telephone had become widely available from the late 1800s, radio broadcasts (*right*) began in the 1920s, and television broadcasts in the 1930s.

At home

In the kitchen

The growth of the cities

Before 1800 most people lived in the country, but by the early part of the 20th century, many people lived in towns and cities. As cities grew more crowded, larger and taller buildings such as the Empire State Building in New York City (*right*) were built for people to live and work in.

The motor car age

Mass production of the Model T Ford (*above left*) from 1913 made it cheaper for ordinary people to buy automobiles. However, wealthy people still bought luxury cars such as the 1931 Bugatti (*below left*).

The changing role of women

Because most men were away fighting during World War I, many women had better paid and more important jobs at this time. After World War I, a further advance for women came when – in some countries – they gained the right to vote for the first time. With better jobs and more money to spend, many women became independent of their families for the first time and were no longer expected to stay at home all their lives to be wives and mothers. This new freedom could be seen in the way the "new" woman looked, with lighter, freer clothes and shorter hair (*left*).

Entertaining everybody

New inventions such as the gramophone, radio and, later, television brought news of events in the rest of the world into people's homes. Many people also enjoyed going out to the movies to see films featuring favorite stars such as Charlie Chaplin (*right*).

WORLD WAR II

After the terrible loss of life in World War I (*see pages 56-57*), people everywhere looked forward to a new and better world. But just over 20 years later the world was plunged into an even more destructive war, a conflict in which 55 million men, women, and children lost their lives.

Among the reasons for the outbreak of this new war were the problems left over from World War I. After the war so many countries were left in debt that during the 1930s there was a worldwide financial crisis that resulted in widespread unemployment and hardship. It was the misery of unemployment that made it easier for two ruthless dictators, Adolf Hitler in Germany and Benito Mussolini in Italy, to seize power. Under their rule, Germany and Italy, along with Japan, soon started to seize other countries' territory. It took more than five years for the Allied forces (who included Britain and the Commonwealth, France, the USSR, and the US) to finally defeat Germany, Italy, and Japan.

1 Retreat from Dunkerque

When France was defeated by Germany in 1940, thousands of British, French, and Belgian troops escaped to the French port of Dunkerque. Here they waded out to boats taking them to safety in England (*below*).

2 The Battle of the Atlantic

After 1940, Britain badly needed supplies from the United States. In the Battle of the Atlantic, German submarines sank ships bringing goods from the US (*above*).

3 The Battle of Britain

During 1940, Germany tried to bomb Britain into defeat. But the Royal Air Force caused such heavy losses among the German aircraft that by the end of 1940, Hitler had put aside his plan of invading Britain.

New types of warfare

By the start of World War II, new improved models of major weapons such as tanks, guns, and aircraft had been introduced. In this war, there was also more use made of spies, saboteurs, and resistance organizations, men and women fighting a "secret" war behind enemy lines.

8 The D-Day landings

Once the Allies had made peace with Italy in 1943, they began to plan the final defeat of Germany. In 1944, on D-Day, American, Canadian, and British armies began the liberation of occupied Europe when they invaded France.

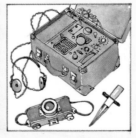

German flying bombs, the V1 and V2, were aimed at British cities for the first time near the end of the war.

Radar, a system of tracking the position of enemy aircraft and ships, was an important weapon throughout the war.

Spies and saboteurs used hidden radios, cameras, and weapons in their work behind the battle lines.

4 Pearl Harbor

Japan's wish to dominate Asia led it to bomb the American Pacific fleet based at Pearl Harbor (*below*), an act that brought the United States into the war on the Allied side in 1941. The Japanese remained victorious in Asia until 1942.

5 The Battle of Stalingrad

The Germans advanced deep into the USSR after their invasion of 1941. But the Soviets fought fiercely to defend cities such as Stalingrad (*below*) and eventually the Germans were driven back.

6 The desert war

For a time, German armies in North Africa were victorious under their brilliant general, Rommel. But the Allies scored their first major success in the war in 1942 when British and Commonwealth troops defeated Rommel (*right*) at Alamein.

7 War in the Pacific

After 1942, the Japanese were slowly driven back in Asia and the Pacific by Allied troops from countries such as the US, Britain, and Australia (*above*).

9 The end of the war

The Germans were finally forced to surrender to the Allies in 1945 after the invasion of Germany and Hitler's suicide. Later, Japan surrendered after the Americans had dropped two atomic bombs (*below*) on Japanese cities.

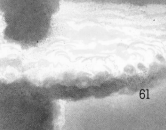

61

THE SPACE AGE

When the American astronaut Neil Armstrong first stepped onto the surface of the moon in 1969, the event was seen throughout the world as a wonderful example of what our modern civilization can achieve. It links us with the explorers of earlier times (*see pages 32-33*).

But the same world that is able to put a man on the moon also finds it difficult to solve some of its most important problems. These include how to feed millions of starving people, how to preserve the world's animals and plants, and, above all, how to prevent wars. It is to be hoped that the great knowledge passed on to us by people who lived in earlier times will help us solve these outstanding problems.

Where people live in the Space Age

As cities have grown larger and more crowded, wealthier city dwellers have often chosen to live in nicer areas away from the city center. But poor people do not have this choice and in many cities they live in dirty, overcrowded areas called slums.

Science in the Space Age

People living in the 20th century have seen many important scientific developments, but since the end of World War II the most dramatic advances have been in the fields of medicine and space travel. New medical advances include the control by vaccine of diseases such as polio, and the ability of surgeons to transplant organs such as the kidneys from one person to another. Extraordinary advances in space travel have resulted in the development of artificial communications satellites, space probes, reusable spacecraft, and crewless space stations.

Acting on the instructions and information they receive, computers (*above*) can now help solve many scientific problems.

Living in the suburbs

People who work in towns or cities often live in communities outside the town center called suburbs, because they want their children to grow up in quieter surroundings, well away from the city's noise and grime.

A wide range of goods

A modern family can own a far wider range of household and leisure goods than families could in earlier times. Many families now have a refrigerator, washing machine, television, and car.

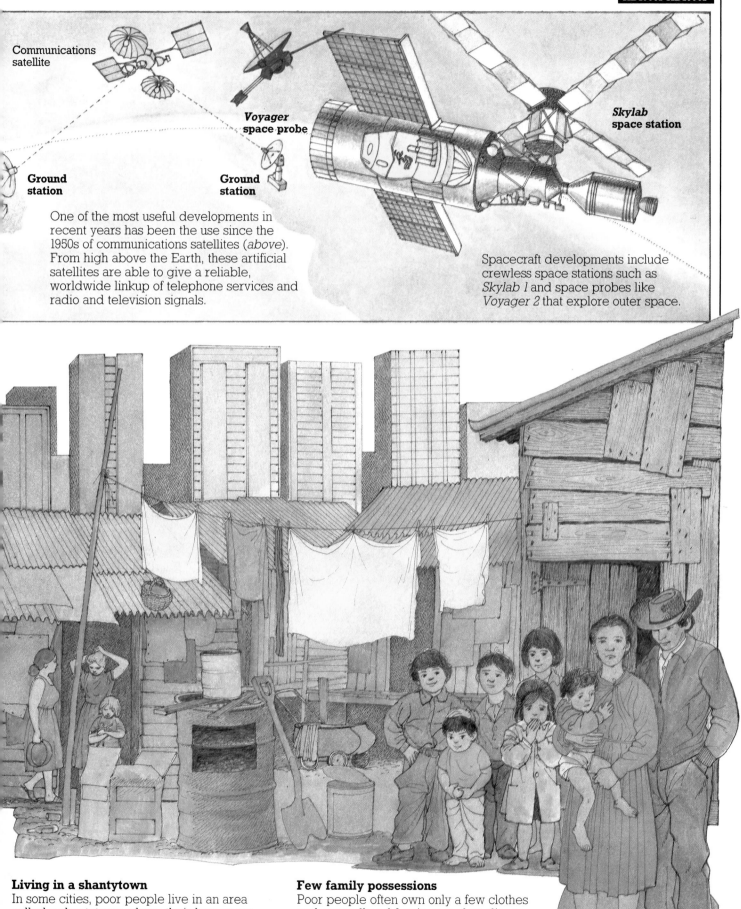

Communications
satellite

Ground
station

Voyager
space probe

Ground
station

Skylab
space station

One of the most useful developments in recent years has been the use since the 1950s of communications satellites (*above*). From high above the Earth, these artificial satellites are able to give a reliable, worldwide linkup of telephone services and radio and television signals.

Spacecraft developments include crewless space stations such as *Skylab 1* and space probes like *Voyager 2* that explore outer space.

Living in a shantytown
In some cities, poor people live in an area called a shantytown where their homes are usually poorly made wooden huts. Shanty-towns often have no water pipes or proper drains, making them unhealthy places to live in.

Few family possessions
Poor people often own only a few clothes and secondhand furniture and appliances. Many poor people have no paid work and find it difficult to feed their children.

INDEX